D1612774

Porsche 924 and 944

Porsche 924 and 944

A collector's guide
by Michael Cotton

MOTOR RACING PUBLICATIONS LTD
Unit 6, The Pilton Estate, 46 Pitlake, Croydon CR0 3RY, England

First Published 1990

British Library Cataloguing in Publication Data

Cotton, Michael *1938–*
   Porsche 924 and 944.
   1. Porsche 924 & 944 cars, history
   I. Title
   629.2222

ISBN 0-947981-46-2

Typeset by
Ryburn Typesetting Ltd, Halifax, West Yorkshire

Printed in Great Britain by
The Amadeus Press Ltd
Huddersfield, West Yorkshire

Contents

Introduction

The first car to wear the Porsche badge, the 356.001 made in 1948, was powered by a nearly standard Volkswagen air-cooled engine developing 35bhp, and the company's range has included at least one four-cylinder model ever since. Porsche's fame and fortune was built upon the 356 model, the last of which was made in 1965, and it was replaced immediately by the 912 coupe which was succeeded in 1969 with the VW-Porsche 914/4 mid-engined model.

The 912 was put back into production for a short period prior to the launch of the Porsche 924, which is where this book begins in 1975. This, too, had a nearly standard VW engine, though water-cooled with 125bhp, having been ordered by Volkswagen as a replacement for the 914/4. In the autumn of 1974 Porsche proposed to buy back the design and launch the car, code-numbered EA 425, as 'a proper Porsche' and although Rudolf Leiding rejected the proposal his successor Toni Schmücker was happy to accept it.

In July 1989, as the model year ended, the 300,000th four-cylinder 'transaxle' Porsche was made in the Audi factory at Neckarsulm. Of these almost exactly half had been 924s (137,500, plus 12,000 924 Turbos) and the remainder 944s powered by Porsche's own 2½-litre, balancer-shaft four-cylinder engines rated as high as 250bhp in turbocharged form.

No longer is there any debate about what actually constitutes 'a proper Porsche'. It is whatever the customer wants it to be, provided of course that it wears the correct badge, but in 1976 the matter was quite controversial and it strained all sorts of relationships within Porsche clubs and between clubs and the manufacturer.

The 924 was no less a Porsche than the most revered and collectable early 356s, but people's perceptions had changed in the meantime. The 356 was unique in 1950, but a quarter of a century later even Ford and Volkswagen could make cars which went quicker than the 924 and cost less. What *they* lacked, as Porsche constantly pointed out, was the shield on the front, a guarantee if you like of excellent engineering, good workmanship and a fine retained value.

Sales of the 924 started at a dizzy level in America and fell sharply in the third year. In Europe on the other hand sales started modestly and built up steadily, a process that proved a boon to the dealer network. The 2-litre 924 changed very little, mechanically, in 10 years, but the process of refinement went on constantly. The original examples were, indeed, noisier and cruder than they should have been, but by 1978 the 924 had matured and become highly regarded by a new clientèle, people who'd never thought before of buying a Porsche. Many of them have stayed loyal to the marque and are driving their 928S-4s even now!

The 170bhp 924 Turbo model was viewed with respect by 911 owners, the 210bhp Carrera GT even more so. The die-hard six-cylinder brigade still couldn't bring themselves to accept the 924 series fully and suspected, rightly, that Prof Dr Ernst Fuhrmann planned to phase the 911 out of production. His replacement, as managing director, by Peter W. Schutz in January 1981 brought about a complete change of emphasis, though.

Schutz, an outgoing American, agreed with Dr Ferry Porsche (today, Professor Porsche) that the 911 is a peerless model that could not be replaced. The V8-powered 928 model was taken further upmarket where it belonged and the four-cylinder series was developed in a way that delighted everyone, with Porsche's own power unit, which was effectively one bank of the V8.

The 944 was seen for the first time at Le Mans in 1981, disguised as a 924 prototype, and has competed with distinction ever since. It has won the Nelson Ledges 24-Hour race in America and survived the rigours of four seasons of one-make racing in the 944 Turbo Cup series. Commercially the 944 has had a bumpy ride, too, starting off with massive demand around the world, losing popularity temporarily as sophisticated developments affected the price lists, then finding its niche out of reach of Japanese challengers.

Technical excellence continues to be the guiding principle for Porsche's entire range, which includes, as ever, a fine selection of four-cylinder models.

Acknowledgements

A book such as this cannot be written without the assistance of the Porsche factory, and I am particularly grateful to many members of the staffs at Weissach and Zuffenhausen for their generous co-operation.

Engineers Jochen Freund, Friedrich Wegert and Thomas Herold were patient in describing the development of the 924 and 944 models from the earliest days. Busier than ever in retirement, Professor Helmuth Bott was kind enough to explain the *philosophies* behind many key developments. In the press office at Zuffenhausen, Manfred Jantke, Klaus Reichert and archivist Klaus Parr were generous, as ever, with their time and facilities. And in Reading, England, support and co-operation was excellent as usual from Jeremy Snook, Corinna Phillips and Melanie Hill.

I am grateful to Bill Oursler, the American 'encyclopaedia' on Porsche and Audi matters, for his invaluable contributions both with information and illustrations; to Betty Jo Turner, editor of *Porsche Panorama* for allowing me to make use of published material, and to Bob Carlson at PCNA for illustrations.

I hope I've done them all justice in preparing this book about the impressive development of Porsche's modern four-cylinder car.

Michael Cotton
Henley-on-Thames
Oxfordshire
February 1990.

CHAPTER 1

The 924 becomes a Porsche

Origins and production

Until 1973, the Porsche company held a contract to develop Volkswagen's products. Professor Ferdinand Porsche himself had designed the original Volkswagen, later known as the Beetle, in the 1930s and even laid out the factory in Wolfsburg, so the connection was very strong indeed. In 1948, his son, Ferdinand 'Ferry' Porsche, shrewdly negotiated not only the supply of Volkswagen components that went into his new type 356 sports car, but to receive a royalty on each Beetle produced and to develop the car and its successors. To ice the cake his sister, Louise Piëch, would handle Volkswagen's distribution arrangements in Austria.

The contract was made in heaven, and it served the house of Porsche handsomely for 25 years. The success of Volkswagen worldwide, and particularly in America, was astonishing, and even as the air-cooled car neared the end of its record-breaking production run in Germany Heinz Nordhoff, 'father' of the Beetle, was able to show 36 potential successors, most of which had been designed and built by Porsche at Zuffenhausen.

When Kurt Lotz succeeded Nordhoff in 1968 he initiated the EA 266 design at Porsche, a family saloon in which a water-cooled flat engine was mounted underneath the back seat, and confirmed the foundation of a new joint-stock company, Volkswagen-Porsche, at Ludwigsburg, to distribute the new type 914 sports car.

Ferdinand Piëch, Dr Porsche's nephew, was in charge of research and development and was responsible for various projects which included the EA 266, the 914/4 (VW engine) and 914/6 (Porsche engine), as well as ongoing development of the 911 model, and production of the awesome type 917 racing car. Busy times indeed!

A severe depression hit the world industry in 1969, of a cyclical nature and led by the decline of the American dollar. It hit Porsche hard, but the Volkswagen-Audi-NSU group suffered even worse as the Beetle went out of fashion and exposed VW's lack of preparedness to produce a successor.

Herr Lotz lasted less than four years before being replaced in September 1971 by Rudolf Leiding. He lost no time in cancelling the EA 266, a blow both for Porsche and Piëch personally, and even ordered the prototypes to be cut up and destroyed. One of the main charges against Nordhoff and Lotz, in turn, was that they hadn't allowed their own R&D department enough latitude, and Leiding answered that by redoubling VW's work on the Golf, and Audi's on the car that became known as the Polo.

As a trade-off Leiding did initiate the development of the EA 425, Volkswagen's replacement for the 914/4 sports car, and Porsche put this in hand early in 1972. Dr Ernst Fuhrmann, designer of the Carrera four-cam engine, was now 'spokesman for the board' at Porsche, effectively heading the company, as Dr Porsche chaired the supervisory board.

Various members of the Porsche and Piëch families were asked in 1971 to seek their futures elsewhere and Ferdinand Piëch found his berth at Audi, where he headed the development team working on the five-cylinder engine and later, the Quattro. Today he heads the Audi company, with a seat on the main board at Volkswagen, which completes the circle for Dr Porsche's nephew. Family connections remained strong, of course, as 10 equal shareholdings in the privately owned Porsche company were held by Dr Porsche and his sister Louise, and the four children of each family.

Neither company, it seemed, liked the VW-Porsche company or its products. Porsche lost interest in 1971 after just 3,107 six-cylinder versions had been built in two years, although 115,600 four-cylinder, VW-powered examples were built by the Karmann company between 1969 and 1975. Such a level of production confirmed that the 914/4 was a success, contrary to popular belief, and America was by far the largest market, accounting for some 15,000 cars a year. It was because of this that the Porsche 912, out of production since 1968, went back into production for the year 1975–76 to bridge the gap until the 924 model came on stream.

It is necessary to run through the history lesson to understand how the Porsche 924 came into being, where it came from, and why. It was developed entirely by Porsche, using as many Volkswagen-Audi parts as possible, and at its heart was the LT four-cylinder, in-line engine. The main debate in 1972 was where to position the engine, and the study ran jointly on this and Porsche's planned 928 model, an upmarket V8 which should break new ground (Fuhrmann saw this as the eventual replacement of the 911 but Dr Porsche thought differently, and eventually it was the main cause of their working relationship breaking down).

The study was carried out by Dipl Ing Helmuth Bott, head of research and development since 1971 and a board member with his base at Weissach, the research centre founded by Porsche on virgin land some 30 kilometres west of Zuffenhausen. He rejected mid- and rear-engined layouts and chose to position the power units longitudinally at the front, a conventional enough solution, but with the gearbox and differential built as one unit (a transaxle) between the rear wheels so as to equalize the weight distribution.

Alfa Romeo, in fact, had already used this layout effectively with the Alfetta, both for racing and road car applications, but the main weakness was the positioning of the clutch at the rear where it suffered from inertial problems (Porsche knew all about these, since the company was being consulted by Alfa Romeo in search of a solution). The answer, as Bott

could see, was to position the clutch in the usual place behind the flywheel, and this line of development was pursued both for the EA 425 and Porsche's own project 928.

The launch of Volkswagen's own Scirocco model in March 1974 indicated that the EA 425 wasn't a main priority, and indeed VW's financial and marketing problems were mounting by the month as a severe recession followed the first oil crisis. In the autumn, Dr Fuhrmann sent his sales director, Lars-Roger Schmidt, to Leiding with a proposal that Porsche should take on the EA 425. 'I got thrown out', Schmidt recalls succinctly, and it seems that Leiding had taken a fancy to the car, and was putting his personal touches to the final design.

Leiding's days at VW were numbered, though. The company was very close to bankruptcy, some of the plants, including Audi's former NSU factory at Neckarsulm, faced closure, and Leiding himself was suffering from ill-health. He resigned in December 1974 and into his place stepped Toni Schmücker.

Schmidt returned to Wolfsburg in January 1975 with the same proposal, and this time it was accepted. 'It wasn't his baby', said Schmidt. 'He had enough problems on his plate and he liked our proposal.' EA 425 was returned to Porsche in February 1975 as an unused package, but another year would pass before production started, appropriately, at Neckarsulm.

Porsche's proposal was to 'buy back' the EA 425, which also had the firm's own type number 924 (although the project started after the 928 it was thought appropriate to use the 4 suffix for four cylinders and 8 for eight cylinders). Rather than pay a fixed sum up front, Porsche would repay the capital on the first 100,000 cars produced. Even so, it would cost Dr Porsche's company DM100 million to take the car in, do the final development work and launch it as a 924. Another item included was the purchase of VW's half-share in the Ludwigsburg operation, winding up the VW-Porsche company. Porsche's own marketing department was then established in Ludwigsburg, which lies just to the north of Stuttgart and a quarter of the way to Neckarsulm.

It was a tough year to find that sort of money, which represented four times the company's average annual investments, and especially since the 1975 model year production, exclusively of 911s, reached an all-time low of 8,618. In itself, though, that production figure merely underlined the pressing need to have a more popular, four-cylinder car in the range. As an added inducement to VW, Porsche needed to have the 924 made in Neckarsulm and this threw a lifeline to the factory, and to the Salzgitter plant where the production of 20,000 extra LT28 engines would come in handy. The engine, incidentally, was also sold in short-block form to American Motors, and was built up in the States to power the oddly-shaped Gremlin.

924 in the making

Dr Ernst Fuhrmann signed the concept document for the 928 in October 1971, on his 53rd birthday as it happened, confirming that it would have a water-cooled V8 engine placed at the front and driving the rear wheels through a transaxle transmission. Simple as this statement may sound, the configuration was the result of an intensive 12-month study carried out by Dipl Ing Helmuth Bott, Porsche's research director, covering 40 criteria.

It was a stroke of luck that three months later Rudolf Leiding gave the go-ahead for the 914/4's replacement, enabling the engineers now installed in an excellent centre at Weissach to do all the experimental work at VW's expense! Project EA 425 (VW) or 924 (Porsche) soon overtook the 928 and the eight-cylinder model was, in any case, delayed later on by the slump of 1974.

Dipl Ing Paul Hensler became the project 'father', in Porsche's terminology the man responsible for co-ordinating the development and making sure it ran to time, and to budget. In styling, a most important aspect, a young Dutchman named Harm Lagaay had his concept picked from the bunch and became responsible for the exterior design,

A BMW 1600 was added to the Weissach fleet in April 1972, due for an even harder life than it had been through previously! It was soon equipped with the 924's intended running gear, notably the 2-metre driveshaft which was still in the experimental stage.

Under the BMW's bonnet was installed the VW-Audi LT four-cylinder, 2-litre engine fitted with a carburettor and developing 95bhp. The BMW was coded 914N, meaning that it was the prototype of the 914's successor.

reporting to styling director Anatole Lapine. In 1988, Lagaay was appointed styling director in succession to Mr Lapine.

A secondhand BMW 1600 was bought in April 1972 and adapted to the intended running gear. The Volkswagen 2-litre engine was carburated and developed 95bhp, in accordance with the contract, and a driveshaft 2 metres in length and 20mm in diameter ran from the clutch back to the Audi four-speed gearbox located in front of the differential.

The BMW was code-numbered 914N, meaning 914 successor, and records kept by project leader Jochen Freund at Weissach show that it went onto the rolling road in October to complete the checks on noise, air flow, engine cooling, transmission efficiency and emissions. By this time an Opel Manta (W1) was on the strength too, with the full 924-specification underfloor including the MacPherson-strut front suspension and 911-style, torsion bar-suspended semi-trailing arms at the rear. Brakes, discs at the front and drums

at the rear, came from VW's parts department, as did the rack-and-pinion steering system, door handles, switches and various other small items.

The first body-in-white was made in June 1973 and was rather more rounded, and Italianate perhaps, than the eventual product. When it was ready for the road the first 924 was already powered by the definitive 2-litre engine, which now had Bosch K-Jetronic injection and developed 125bhp; the emission-controlled version for America developed 110bhp. The engine departed from VW's standard in having a revised cylinder head, new inlet and exhaust manifolding to suit the injection system and a larger oil pump, but nothing below the cylinder head line was changed.

It was Rudolf Leiding who determined the final shape, which is to his great credit. 'We showed it to the Volkswagen board', says Freund, 'and Mr Leiding made a lot of changes. He was a hobby stylist and he wanted to give the car its final

Following the BMW onto the fleet was an Opel Manta, coded W1, another sorry-looking car that wouldn't attract attention. It, too, was largely rebuilt from VW's parts bin.

The Opel was noteworthy because it was powered by the Bosch fuel-injected 2-litre engine rated at 125bhp, the definitive 924 engine in all but a few details.

Harm Lagaay, a promising young Dutchman on Tony Lapine's styling staff, produced the most promising design for the 924, the one that was adopted and developed.

Lagaay's 924 prototype was built in June 1973 and seemed to be more rounded and Italianate than the eventual production model. Remarkably few changes were made in the final stages of development.

look.' What Leiding wanted, and got, was a less bulbous appearance.

The crease along the sides was accentuated, the wheelarches were increased in size and radius, the rear side windows were altered and the rear hatch glass was extended. Changed, too, were the rear lights, which became the focal point of the back of the car, with coloured glass running full-width from either side of the number-plates. The bumper blades were nodded through, these being glassfibre inserts mounted on aluminium tubular structures which would deform in a 5mph impact.

Leiding and the VW board finally signed-off the design late in the summer of 1974, but a few months later Toni Schmücker took up the reins and in February 1975 the

project officially became the Porsche 924. The 95bhp carburated 2-litre engine was ditched without ceremony, but another year went by before Audi could tool up the Neckarsulm factory to produce the car on Porsche's behalf.

It was a virtue of the Porsche 924 that it carried a surprising amount of luggage, always a criticism of the 911. The two occasional seats at the rear were quite adequate for young children, and behind them was a wide 'rear deck' which could accommodate two full-size suitcases, although the floor was rather high on account of the transmission. When the rear seats were folded down flat the 924 became a sporty estate car, a versatility greatly appreciated by many customers.

At one stage, when Porsche's own five-speed gearbox was

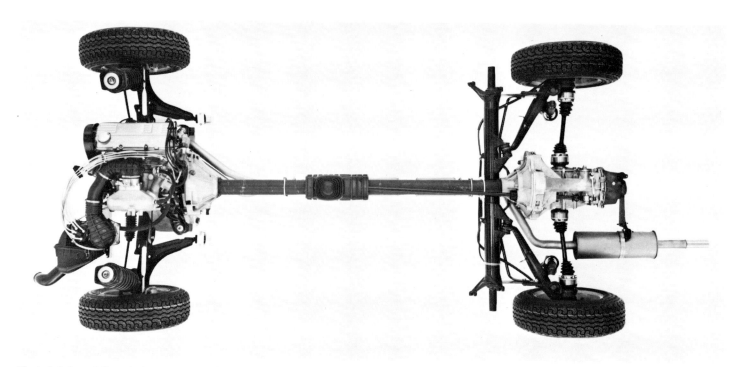

First sighting of Porsche's new transaxle system was in 1975 when the 924 was announced; scaled up, a similar system would also be used in the 928 model, which had been delayed by the 1974 slump.

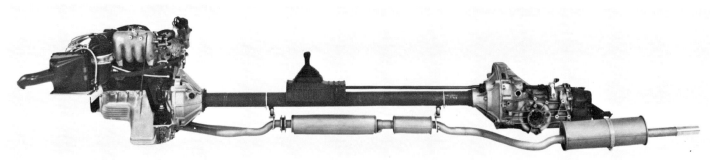

The 'backbone' transaxle allowed a nearly equal weight distribution to be achieved. The Audi gearbox has a bulky clutch-housing which is empty, because Porsche positioned the clutch at the front to reduce inertial forces.

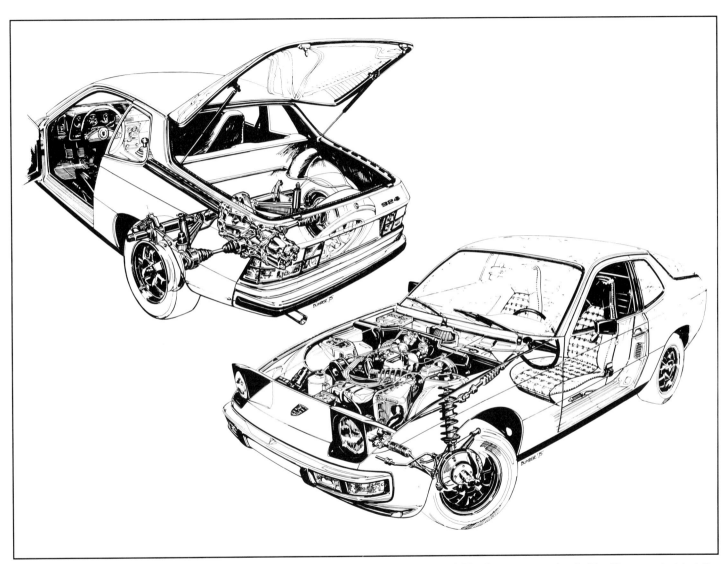

Two cutaway views of the 924 model announced in 1975 (but not built until early '76). The front suspension is MacPherson strut but the rear suspension is by transverse torsion bars, economical with space and more conventionally Porsche.

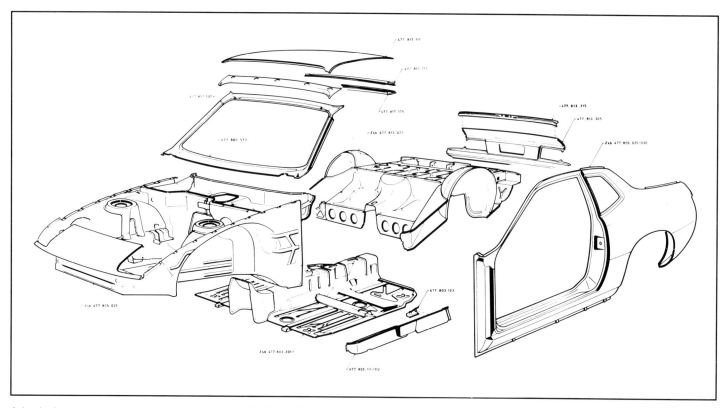

A bodyshop parts department diagram, with all the main panels prefixed 477. The steel body was largely galvanized, and even original examples of the 924 can be found in excellent condition.

fitted in 1978–79 as an option, the Weissach engineers planned to take advantage of its compactness to lower the floor. 'Our gearbox does not have space for the clutch, you see', explained Herr Freund, 'so it was much smaller. If we had lowered the floor there would have been more space for the rear seats, more legroom and more space for the luggage as well.'

The Porsche box, though, was really intended just for the forthcoming Turbo model and the 924 continued to use the much less expensive Audi transmission as standard. The decision was made easier when Audi made the gearbox stronger and added the fifth gear.

A feature of the 924 was its wind-cheating shape, and the two-plus-two boasted a low drag coefficient of 0.36 at the outset. It also had high overall gearing with a differential ratio of 9/31 (3.4444) ensuring that the noise levels were low and the fuel consumption was good.

In Britain an average of 30mpg would be considered typical, dipping to 27mpg perhaps when driven very hard, or in heavy traffic. Contributing to the low drag figure, of

In 1975 this production prototype was photographed, without the Porsche badge. Detailed examples of tidying-up have improved the car's appearance since the prototype stage, notably removing some of the bulbous lines, filling the wheelarches, tidying up the glassfibre collapsible bumper blades, and introducing a lip to the front air dam.

Steel wheels were standard equipment for the early 924s, along with metal-backed mirrors, which turned rusty at an alarming rate.

This example, with production badging, has the alloy wheels which quickly became standard in most markets. Tail-end treatment was very tidy, with neatly integrated lamps and a complete absence of superfluous ornament.

Retractable headlamps were elevated by an electric motor when required. The driving lamps in the front bumper could be used for daytime signalling.

Many of the early factory photos were taken on the French Riviera, where the 924 was launched, and there were endless opportunities to associate the car with wealth.

course, was the sleek nose profile with the radiator opening hidden away below the number-plate, while the headlamps were concealed in electrically powered pods.

As for the performance, an honest maximum speed of 200km/h (125mph) was claimed, and the car would accelerate from a standstill to 100km/h (62.1mph) in 10.5 seconds. That was a pessimistic figure really since British magazine testers easily broke 10 seconds in the sprint to 60mph, and *Motor*'s equipment recorded 8.2 seconds, surely an optimistic mark.

The handling was widely praised, as it deserved, because it had the usual Porsche pedigree plus the advantage of a nearly equal weight distribution, 53:47 front:rear with half a tank of fuel. On the negative side, the 924 was criticized for having a somewhat harsh ride, with marked 'bump-thump' from the tyres, a noisy fuel pump, chatter from the main driveshaft when the car was in neutral, and a lower level of refinement than people were accustomed to from Porsche. Obviously the engineers at Weissach had more work to do, tasks that they had perhaps expected Volkswagen's staff to undertake.

Some of the early examples used in the launch and in early production (February to July 1976) were characterized by some rather flashy check-patterned upholstery, but by the time the UK-market cars were built with right-hand drive, for delivery early in 1977, the interiors were more sober with pin-stripe or tweed-flecked upholstery.

Most of the 5,145 Porsche 924s built before the summer break were reserved for the German domestic market, but the 924 was launched in the States in July 1976 and found a ready market. Records kept by Porsche Cars North America show that 4,544 were sold by the end of December, and the rate of sale continued to climb steadily in the first half of 1977. More than 1,500 were sold each month in April, May and June and the 1977 year-end total reached 13,696.

It looked impressive on paper, but those with the figures at their fingertips realized that sales dwindled after August, and only reached four figures again in the same three months of 1978. In the full calendar year of 1978 the Porsche-Audi division of Volkswagen moved 10,483 924s, the following year 8,387, and just over 5,200 in 1980 and in 1981. In six years the US market accounted for 50,034 four-cylinder Porsches and the feeling was that the Mazda RX-7, and to a lesser extent the Datsun 240Z, had stolen the market. The Mazda even had similar styling when it came out early in 1978, and nobody worried about the fuel consumption when the price was substantially lower than Porsche's.

A different picture was painted in Europe and other world markets, where the 924 model made a slow start but then accelerated gradually. Early in the 1977 calendar year Porsche made a special series of 'Martini' 924s, ostensibly to celebrate the double world championships earned by the Martini & Rossi-sponsored 935 and 936 racing cars.

Perhaps the 911 customers would have liked a special edition too, but the marketing department had its shoulder to the wheel and 1,000 924s were made in white with blue and red 'Martini' stripes along the sides, scarlet pile carpets, white enamelled alloy wheels, anti-roll bars at the front and rear, a leather-trimmed steering wheel and a commemorative plaque. Colourful they may sound, but the Martini Porsche 924s were very nice cars, which have tended to command a small premium ever since.

Total production of the 924 model reached 23,180 in the 1977 model year (September 1976 to August 1977), making it the most successful Porsche ever produced; not at any price would Porsche allow the 914/4s to be included in their totals, but in any case the 924 was a stronger seller in its first year. In the second model year, to August 1978, a further 21,000 were made, taking the total past 50,000 in just 26 months.

Refinement was an ongoing process, and the first noteworthy modification for the 1978 model year was to mount the rear suspension arms with rubber bushes, reducing the interior noise level markedly. There was less vibration, less harshness, but a little more compliance in the rear, which didn't impair the 924's handling in any way.

Porsche's own five-speed transmission, as used in the earlier 911 models, was offered as an option for those who wanted closer ratios, although fifth was no higher than fourth in Audi's four-speed box. The mass-produced transmission wasn't strong enough to take any more power, and Porsche wanted to 'run in' their own box in preparation for the launch

Compared with the 924 prototype shots, the bumper blades are much tidier with a wraparound shape. They are mounted on collapsible aluminium structures, good enough for the 5mph impact test and cheaper than the 911's shock-absorbing system.

The best view of the 924, some would say, showing off the clean styling which, like all of Porsche's designs, has stood the test of time.

Two right-hand-drive prototypes arrived in Britain a few days before the 1976 Motor Show at Earls Court, and orders were taken for first deliveries in January 1977, priced at £6,999 ('very expensive' commented *Motor*). The show cars were painted Minerva Blue and Reseda Green.

of the 924 Turbo.

Audi made this redundant when the 1980 model year cars went down the line, as the mass-produced box was uprated and had a fifth gear added. As a bonus, it was a much nicer transmission to operate than Porsche's, as customers soon found. British market customers, sitting on the right, always found that Porsche's box was difficult to use, with first gear positioned awkwardly to the left.

Audi's three-speed automatic transmission had been available since the start of the 1977 calendar year, but the 924's performance was thoroughly disappointing, the 0–60mph figure remaining stubbornly on the wrong side of 11 seconds. It was supposed that the people who bought 924 automatics wouldn't be interested in checking their accelerative powers against those of a Ford Escort, or a Volkswagen Golf.

American customers were disappointed with the

The 2-litre engine, inclined 30 degrees to the right, is equipped with Bosch K-Jetronic injection. Throughout the life of the standard 924, from 1975 to 1985, the power unit was left strictly alone.

performance level, too, their 55mph overall speed limit in no way inhibiting their desire to accelerate strongly. Possibly this was a key to falling sales, and Weissach raised the power of the emission-controlled version from 110 to 115bhp for the 1978 model year, but to little avail.

Mechanically, the 2-litre 924 model was virtually unchanged in 10 years. The engine delivered 125bhp throughout at 5,800rpm and 164.8Nm of torque (121.5lb/ft) at 3,500rpm. The Weissach team never neglected to refine the car, but modifications were, often as not, the result of development on the 924 Turbo model.

In August 1977 (1978 model year) the 924 was given

uprated shock absorbers, which went with the rubber-bushed rear suspension mountings, electric window lifters were offered optionally (to a huge cheer from the dealer network!), black enamelled alloy wheels with polished rims became a popular option – the rough-finished cast-alloy wheels were particularly prone to discolouring from the brake dust – and, a minor but distinctive detail, the exhaust system tailpipe was made oval, with a better finish.

Two years went by before the next batch of improvements became available. These included the standardization of the Audi five-speed gearbox with fifth on the right, opposite reverse, the brake servo increased in size from 7 to 9 inches

Perhaps the dashboard was the least attractive part of the 924, with Volkswagen instruments sunk into a plastic facia. The dashboards were prone to creaking, and the 'tartan' seat covers were considered flashy. Note, too, the eccentric steering wheel, which failed to answer criticism about knee-room.

for lighter pressures, electric control for the exterior mirrors, and an automatic light in the luggage compartment. The 1980 model was distinguished by 'black look' window frames, and a hinged flap in body colour over the black VW fuel filler cap.

Across the board, Porsche completed its anti-corrosion programme (already the best in the world) in the summer of 1980, extending the warranty against rust perforations to seven years. The 924 was the main beneficiary here because the entire body was galvanized where previously only the floor and wheelarches had been fully protected.

More soundproofing was introduced, and to improve the car's handling still further the rear torsion bars were made stiffer and the front anti-roll bar was standardized. Air horns, from the Turbo model, were also standardized, a foglamp was added at the rear and turn indicator repeaters on the sides of the front wheelarches. Optional equipment included attractive (but difficult to clean) spoke-effect alloy wheels, still with four-stud fixings, full cloth or leather trim seats, and a cassette box in the centre armrest.

By now the 924 model had settled down to a very modest existence in America, averaging 300–400 sales a month; even the 26-strong British Porsche dealer network was able to reach that number in a good month. The car was popular in Italy, too, where the 2-litre tax-break worked strongly in its favour, and it didn't do badly in France, Austria and Switzerland.

The announcement of a 'Le Mans' model immediately followed the sixth-place finish of the 924 GTR model in the 1980 Le Mans race, finished in Alpine White with discreet red, yellow and black coachlines along the sides. This series had black leather seats with white piping, uprated dampers, front and rear anti-roll bars, 6J x 15 spoke-effect alloy wheels with 205/60 VR tyres, and a smaller 36cm diameter four-spoke leather steering wheel. The addition of the Turbo model's polyurethane spoiler around the rear window was enough, apparently, to reduce the drag coefficient by three points to 0.33, and today this is very much a collectable model.

There was quite a celebration in Zuffenhausen early in

A 'Martini' special edition of the 924 was on sale in spring of 1977 (not long after the rhd launch), celebrating two world championship crowns earned by Porsche the previous year. All 1,000 cars were painted white, had attractive Martini stripes and deeper pile, scarlet carpets.

1981, and at Neckarsulm too, as the 100,000th Porsche 924 was produced. The contract with Volkswagen-Audi was finally fulfilled, four years and 11 months after production started, and both parties had reason to feel extremely satisfied with the bargain. The going hadn't been altogether easy for Porsche in the American market but the 924 had reached expectations everywhere else, and all the elements except the engine were well proven for the next-generation model, the 944, due for announcement in June 1981.

In August 1981, the 924 benefited from an improved ventilation system with a stronger through-flow, in common with the new 944, but this was criticized for blowing warm air through the facia vents in the wintertime. The 924 now had the 911-style three-spoke leather steering wheel as standard. Twelve months later, as the Turbo went out of production, the 924 was given the polyurethane rear spoiler as standard, soundproofing was further improved, and the interior was uprated to the same standard as the 944 model.

Synchromesh was fitted to reverse gear.

As the 924 went into its ninth year production topped 130,000, and some minor improvements were announced in common with the 944: the sunroof had an electric tilt mechanism, there was an electrically operated release button inside the car for the rear hatch (at last!), easier control for seat backrest adjustment, and the name 'Porsche' was woven into the cloth seat material.

Finally, 7,500 924s were made in the 1985 model year exclusively for European markets, taking the full total to 137,500. The only modifications of note were the addition of heated windscreen washer nozzles and a screen with gradual darkening of the tinting. Now a thoroughly sophisticated car, it was ready for Porsche's own 2½-litre counterbalanced engine, which turned it into a 924S for the 1986 model year.

Epic runs
Once a Porsche factory racing driver, Austrian Rudi Lins

The Austrians Rudi Lins and Gerhard Plattner began a whole series of publicized proving runs in the 924, this one in 1976 covering 22,313 trouble-free kilometres across five continents in 28 days.

turned his hand to marathon driving in the 1970s. His partner, Gerhard Plattner, was the public relations manager for Porsche in Salzburg, so their credentials with the factory, and with the engineers in Weissach, were very strong.

In the space of 12 months their standard Porsche 924 covered 80,000 kilometres, the likes of which hadn't been tackled before. Their first feat was to follow the steps of Jules Verne's Phileas Fogg and to drive around the world, not in 80 days but in 28. Their route, on land, traversed five continents and put 22,313 kilometres onto the odometer, apparently without any major problems at all.

Later in 1976, when the car had been 'tested' by a large number of journalists, it was driven at high speed up and down the Brenner autobahn for 100 hours, averaging 71.8mph and 28.0 miles per gallon. The third epic, undertaken in January–February 1977 in the same car, involved driving from the world's northernmost town, Hammerfest, to the most southern, Ushuaia in Argentina, a distance of 32,000kms.

Apart from a shock absorber, damaged in a heavy landing

Inevitably the German Polizei had to have the latest in Porsches, though the company's PR department made sure that everyone knew. With a maximum speed of 200km/h the 924 was a match for most on the autobahns.

Another special version of the 924 was prepared at Weissach for the 'flying doctor' service, designed to arrive rapidly at the scene of autobahn pile-ups or other disasters.

28

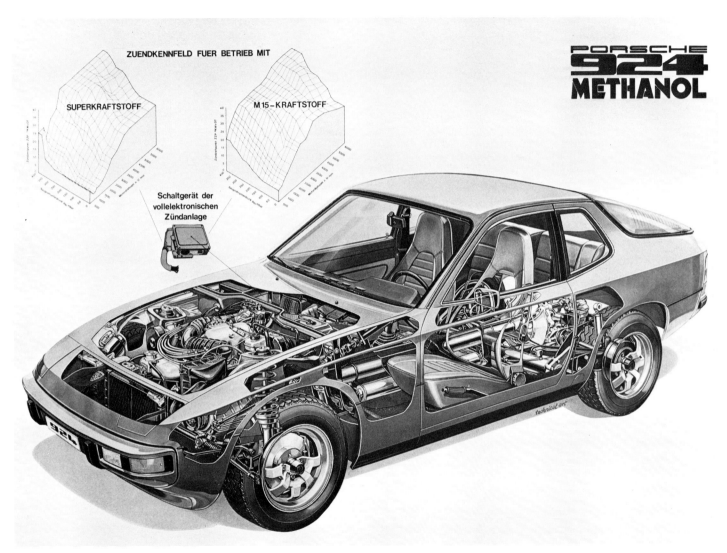

ZUENDKENNFELD FUER BETRIEB MIT

SUPERKRAFTSTOFF

M15–KRAFTSTOFF

Schaltgerät der
vollelektronischen
Zündanlage

PORSCHE
924
METHANOL

A special series of 924s was prepared at Weissach to run on a methanol mixture as part of a government-sponsored research scheme into alternative fuels in the late 1970s. The power output rose slightly to 130bhp, but plastic parts in the fuel system had to be replaced by other materials.

near Santa Fe, there were no breakages on the car at all. Temperatures ranged from minus 40°C in the Arctic Circle to plus 40°C in South America, and the highest altitude reached was 13,000 feet (4,265 metres) in the Andes. Even the Austrians seem to have been surprised that the long-suffering Porsche had no technical problems. Main sponsors Mobil, Dunlop and Bosch should have been pleased, too, as the car went the whole way on the same sump of SHC oil, and not one of the SP 66 MS winter tyres needed changing between the Capes.

Later on, Lins and Plattner would undertake difficult journeys in the 924 Turbo, the 928 and 944 models. Another remarkable accomplishment was with the 944S (16-valve) in 1987, Plattner covering 384,405 kilometres (238,861 miles), which happens to be the return distance from Earth to the Moon. 'There were never any problems with the engines, gearbox, shock absorbers, nothing', Jochen Freund confirms. 'We wanted to do this distance with one car just to see what happens.' Three engines were installed, not because any wore out but because the Weissach engineers wanted to test new

Early in 1977 a roller-blind was introduced to the 924's specification to cover luggage lying in the boot. The luggage capacity was 4.8 cubic feet, rising to 7.7cu ft with the rear seat back folded flat.

For the 1978 model year rubbing strips were placed along the flanks of the 924, and the exterior mirror design was improved with damage-resistant backing, and heated glass with interior adjustment. Also for 1978 the rear suspension arms were rubber-mounted to reduce vibration and noise, a refinement that made the 924 a far better car. Porsche's own five-speed gearbox became available optionally and was used on the 924 Championship track car series. For the 1980 model year Audi's own five-speed gearbox (a much nicer transmission) was standard equipment.

Favourite numbers adopted by Porsche Cars Great Britain were 924 F and 924 DLC. This is the 1980 model (from September 1979) featuring the flap over the petrol filler cap. Black-centre alloy wheels were popular, and ongoing development had transformed the 924 since the early days. If buying today, start with this model.

parts in real-life conditions, one of them being the 3-litre that was announced a year later. The air bag system was tested, too, though not in an accident.

A total of 71 drivers handled the 944S, including Freund, and the car criss-crossed northern America before being flown to Germany for the bulk of its travel. The lunar distance was covered in just nine months, and the test continued to the 500,000 kilometre mark within 12 months. Tyre equipment, this time, was supplied by Pirelli, who wanted the P700 endurance-tested, and Shell supplied the TMO oil.

Durability is something one expects to take for granted in a modern car, especially a Porsche, but least of all can a company like Porsche get complacent about the longevity of every component that goes into a complex vehicle.

So concerned was the world about fuel consumption in the 1970s that the German government sponsored a national programme for research into alternative fuels. Each German motor manufacturer played its part, Porsche contributing a fleet of 10 924s adapted to run on methanol. Compressions

A British-market 'Lux' option in 1980 was the 911's steering wheel, along with twin electrically operated exterior mirrors and a Panasonic radio/cassette player.

were raised substantially, from 9.3 to 12.5:1, and 15% of methanol was added to each measure of gasoline. The findings were certainly encouraging. The engines were slightly more powerful, at 130bhp, but ran cooler and with lower emissions, and were more economical, too. The engines would, in fact, run just as well on aethanol, a fuel produced biologically from beetroot, sugar cane or cereals. However, the fuel system had to be modified and plastic parts replaced.

On a parallel course, Porsche experimented with the Thermo-dynamically Optimum Porsche (TOP) high-efficiency cylinder head. Compressions were raised to between 11:1 and 13:1, the combustion chamber shape was changed to induce greater 'swirl', and the air:fuel ratio was leaned off. None of this saw the light of day in the 924, but was of immense value for the 944 design.

S is sweeter

In calendar time we have to jump three years, from the launch of the 944 model to the debut of the 924S, which used the same 2,479cc engine. It had been intended, back in 1980, to launch the 944 model with the 'narrow' 924 bodyshell, but soon after Peter Schutz's arrival in January 1981 the plan was changed. The incoming chief executive looked at, and liked

From September 1980 the front wings carried indicator repeaters, as required by law in some countries, and a rear foglight was added. The front anti-roll bar became standard with stiffer torsion bars at the rear.

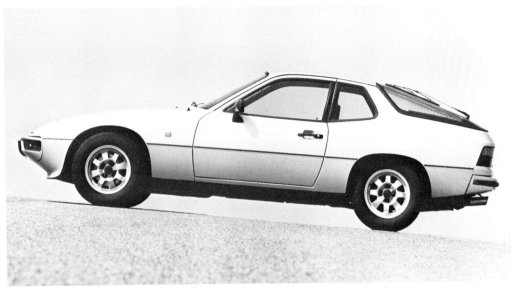

With the demise of the 924 Turbo in 1982 its polyurethane rear window wraparound spoiler was fitted to the 924 model, lowering the drag figure by three points (0.33). Also to be noted in the photo (author driving) are the optional spoke-effect alloy wheels, still with four-stud fixings, the first alternative to the rather ugly wheels of the earlier versions.

In September 1984 the 2-litre 924 went into its final year with many refinements common to the 944 model. There was a remote-control release for the rear window (not before time), electric tilt for the sunroof, and heated washer nozzles. Subtly, and without spending much money, Porsche had kept the 924 model looking young throughout the ten years of production.

Something that fascinates the Continentals is a car's ability to cover 1,000 kilometres on a tank of fuel. This 'discreetly' liveried 2-litre 924 ran the distance on German autobahns in 1983 with the standard 66-litre tank, averaging 6.6 litres per 100kms, or 42.7mpg.

The 924S model was announced midway through 1985, finally succeeding the 2-litre model. The 2.5-litre balancer-shaft engine was slightly detuned to 150bhp (110kW), and the model was distinguished by 928-type alloy wheels with five-stud fixings. With a drag coefficient of 0.33, the 2½-litre Porsche 924S had a top speed of 135mph and, with the narrow body, was not much slower than the more powerful 944. The suspensions were now made of aluminium and full disc braking was installed, like that on the 944. The 924's original dashboard style was retained, though.

the Carrera GT model and decided that the 944 should follow the style. The outline was already on the drawing boards intended for the 944 Turbo, due in 1984, but Schutz had the 'wide body' style brought forward at express speed.

'It was a difficult time for us', says Ing Freund, a man who has been with Porsche's four-cylinder cars from the first days of the 924, in 1971, through to the present-day 944S and Turbo. 'We had confusing signals from the board of management . . . so many things were started, and stopped again.' In the summer of 1985, the 924S became what many engineers had expected the 944 to be. On account of the narrower body the 924S had the potential to be faster and more economical than the 944, a matter which could have proved embarrassing. It was resolved by lowering the

compression ratio from 10.6:1 to 9.7:1, knocking the power down from 163bhp to 150bhp.

It was more to the point, perhaps, that the 924S could run on low-octane, lead-free fuel and still develop its quota of power with catalytic equipment installed, whereas the 944 lost 8bhp and was quoted at 155bhp for controlled markets. Even without a catalyst, though, a good 924S was still on a par with an average 944 although it lost out somewhat in corners, on narrower wheels.

Compared with the 2-litre 924, the new version was a quantum leap ahead. The engine, with 25bhp more to offer and a sackful of torque – more than 130lb/ft across the best part of the engine's range, peaking at 144lb/ft – was smooth to 6,500rpm (or more) where the 2-litre engine was decidedly

Originally launched with 150bhp, the 924S engine later boasted 160bhp, a figure also claimed with full emission equipment in place.

unhappy.

In terms of performance, the 924S was 10mph faster than the 2-litre with a maximum of 135mph, and decidedly quicker in acceleration. From standstill to 60mph, for instance, took 7.8 seconds against an average of 9.6sec for the predecessor, and it accelerated to 100mph in 22.9 seconds, something like 10 seconds quicker. On the downside, though, the average fuel consumption was between 22 and 26mpg, decidedly inferior to the 924's. The 2-litre 924 had been held below the £10,000 price level in the UK between 1978 and 1980 and deserved its popularity, but in the mid-1980s prices were beginning to move up rapidly. A well-equipped 924 could be ordered for £13,000 in 1984, but the 924S carried very little extra equipment, not even a passenger door mirror, when it was introduced at £15,000 in the autumn of 1985.

Certainly the 944 cost £17,551, but it was better-equipped and had the later-styled dashboard, not to mention extra power and wider wheels. The 924S was on a tough mission, and to make its life a little easier it was given another 10bhp

36

Not until 1988 did the 'narrow' body of the original 924 undergo any modification, and here the 160bhp 924S model is seen with the polyurethane air dam skirt characteristic of this model only.

At the rear, the last 924S models made were equipped with the rear underbody diffusers common to the 944S, improving the airflow under the car and introducing a modicum of ground effect.

for the 1988 model year.

In a realignment of the four-cylinder range, the 924S was rated up to 160bhp and the base 944 down to the same figure, though the 160 mark was maintained with emission controls; those who wanted more power were expected to order the 16-valve 944S, or the Turbo.

The price of the 924S had risen sharply to £21,000 as the 160bhp version became available in the autumn of 1987, but the performance level hadn't improved commensurately. The 0–60mph time was lowered to 7.4 seconds, according to *Motor*, the 0–100mph time fell to 20.1 seconds and the maximum speed went up to 137.1mph.

They were good figures, but perhaps not good enough. Sales in America remained stubbornly around the 3,000 mark per year and in the summer of 1988 the 924 model was laid to rest (*Motor* magazine broke the news with brutal honesty on July 9, 1988: 'Porsche 924 is dead'). Even with Porsche's own balancer-shaft engine the road-test experts never really overcame their early prejudices, although the similar 944 was judged in a different way.

CHAPTER 2

Porsche's new turbo baby

A boost for the 924

In 1978, the Porsche Turbo – the vaunted 911 Turbo, that is – was still a relative youngster which had been on the market for three years. Porsche hadn't pioneered turbocharging, but had demonstrated that it could turn even a high-performing car such as the 3-litre 911 into a personal rocket. Maximum speeds of 150mph, and accelerations to 100mph in under 14 seconds, came within reach of many people who were accustomed to much less exciting levels of performance.

While the 924 was struggling for acceptance the management decided to apply the new technique of turbocharging to a special version. The decision was taken in 1976 and two years later, in the spring of 1978, the 924 Turbo was announced with a power output of 170bhp. Production began in the summer, early for the 1979 model year, and immediately the Porschephiles asserted that 'this is what the 924 should have been from the beginning'. So it wasn't the origin of the engine that was the bugbear, but its relative lack of sparkle.

It was recognized that the crankcase, crankshaft and general bottom-end arrangements of the LT engine were quite adequate for a lot more power, but the oil flow was increased considerably and lubricant was sprayed underneath the new forged-alloy pistons as an aid to cooling; an external oil cooler was added, air being ducted to this from four characteristic grilles cut into the front apron.

There were two more grilles hidden away underneath the spotlights, serving the brakes, and finally a NACA duct in the bonnet, to the right of centre looking from the driver's seat, served to lower the under-bonnet temperature.

An entirely new cylinder head was prepared for the turbocharged version, made of alloy and with the platinum-tipped spark plugs moved closer to the inlet valves, which were 3mm larger than those in the 924. The nominal compression ratio was reduced to 7.5:1, rising geometrically to 10.8:1 when the KKK turbocharger was on full boost – 0.7bar (9.87 pounds) from 2,800rpm.

Paul Hensler, Porsche's head of powertrain development, pointed out at the launch in 1978 that it was the development at Weissach of the turbocharger pressure control mechanism, the wastegate, that made it suitable for passenger car application. The turbocharger spins at 100,000rpm and no difficulties were expected with the system.

The Bosch K-Jetronic injection system was recalibrated to supply more fuel to match the greater flow of air, and a secondary fuel pump was installed to raise the delivery pressure (this was also fitted to the 924 model, though only as a convenience). Power was increased by 36% to 170bhp at 5,500rpm, torque by an even more impressive 48%, from 121.5lb/ft to 180lb/ft at the same engine speed, 3,500rpm.

This made it necessary to increase the size of the clutch from 215mm to 225mm, and at the same time it was converted to hydraulic control; the longitudinal driveshaft was increased in diameter from 20 to 25mm, and was then so much more rigid that it ran in three bearings instead of four; a Porsche five-speed gearbox was installed in place of the Audi transmission, and the driveshafts were made stronger.

Significantly, Porsche's own hubs and bearings were fitted, and this made it possible to fit ventilated discs at the front

Porsche's 924 Turbo was announced in the spring of 1978, still with 2-litre capacity but now boasting 170bhp. The five-stud spoke-effect alloy wheels denote 911 hubs, a full disc brake system and stiffened suspension. Four vents above the bumper increase the air flow to the larger radiator, and slots in the air dam feed air to the front brakes.

A NACA duct in the bonnet is another way of reducing under-bonnet temperatures, and a rubber air dam underneath the engine helps to extract air while the car is moving.

From this angle there is little to distinguish the turbocharged car from the normal 924. The leading features are the polyurethane spoiler round the rear window, which actually has a large effect in reducing the drag figure from 0.36 to 0.33, and the five-stud spoke-effect alloy wheels.

Extra air intakes are an immediate giveaway to the 170bhp Turbo version of the 924, and some attractive two-tone colour schemes were introduced for the launch series. The Turbo's spring and damper rates were increased, more than was necessary to cope with an extra 29kg of weight over the front wheels. Anti-roll bars were standardized front and rear, sport dampers were offered as an option, but lower-geared steering spoiled the effect a little.

and rear with the 928's floating calipers. The wheels, which went up from 14 to 15 inches in diameter, had the 911's five-stud fixings and adopted the spoke-effect design.

This wasn't just a bolt-on turbocharger by any stretch of the imagination. The Turbo model was reworked from front to back with Bilstein gas dampers instead of Boge hydraulic, a 9-inch brake servo instead of a 7-inch unit (that too was incorporated in the 924 specification a year later), and even such details as a rubber spoiler underneath the engine shield, creating a low-pressure area to extract hot air from the engine

and front brakes.

The engine was built by Porsche at Zuffenhausen, rather than by VW at Salzgitter, and trucked up to Neckarsulm where the finishing touches were put to a very different type of 924. There was still the feeling that visually it was 'just a 924', and to take the Turbo model as far away from standard as possible two-tone paintwork was offered. Opinions vary, but red or blue over silver, or dark green over light green, made some very attractive combinations.

At last the 924 was a real sports car, in the proper manner.

It had truly competitive acceleration, from rest to 100km/h (62.1mph) in 7.8 seconds, and covering the standing kilometre in 28.0 seconds. As for the top speed, it would reach a genuine 140mph (225km/h), enabling the four-cylinder model to hold its own with almost anything on the autobahn. New, too, was the polyurethane spoiler around the back window, lowering the drag coefficient by one point to 0.35 and contributing to the higher mean speed.

There was a very small weight penalty of 50kg, all at the front end, unfortunately, since the Porsche gearbox was lighter and couldn't therefore make any compensation. Since the design specified a smaller-diameter steering wheel, the steering rack was given a lower ratio of 20:1 (instead of 19:1), and for many this was a small blemish on an otherwise outstanding specification.

At the time of the announcement, PCGB prepared a list of leading modifications, and for the purpose of describing the 924 Turbo model it is self-explanatory:

	924 Coupe	924 Turbo
Engine	4-cylinder, 4-stroke in-line, water-cooled	4 cylinder, 4-stroke in-line, water-cooled with KKK turbocharger
Bore	86.5mm	86.5mm
Stroke	84.4mm	84.4mm
Capacity	1,984cc	1,984cc
Compression	9.3:1	7.5:1
Ignition	Bosch coil and distributor	Bosch contactless transistorized
Max power	125bhp @ 5,800rpm	170bhp @ 5,500rpm USA, 150 @ 5,500rpm
Max torque	121.5lb/ft at 3,500rpm	180lb/ft at 3,500rpm
Valves	Overhead, driven by vee belt	Overhead, driven by vee belt
Lubrication	Pressurized oil system	Pressurized oil system with modified sump, plus oil cooler
Exhaust	Normal	KKK turbocharger
Fuel Octane	98 ROZ	98 ROZ

Chassis		
Front suspen	Independent, wishbones, MacPherson struts, Boge dampers, 22mm anti-roll bar	Independent, wishbones, MacPherson struts, Bilstein dampers, 23mm anti-roll bar
Rear suspen	Independent, transverse torsion bars, Boge dampers, 18mm anti-roll bar	Independent, transverse torsion bars, Bilstein dampers, 14mm anti-roll bar
Steering	Rack-and-pinion, ratio 19.1:1, 383mm diameter wheel	Rack-and-pinion, ratio 20:1, 378mm diameter wheel
Brakes	Hydraulic, twin-circuit with diagonally opposed braking, 7-inch servo Front: solid discs, 257mm diameter Rear: drums, 240mm diameter	Hydraulic, twin-circuit with diagonally opposed braking, 9-inch servo Front: ventilated discs, 282mm diameter Rear: ventilated discs 289mm diameter
Wheels	6J x 14 pressure cast alloy, 4-stud fixing	6J x 15 pressure cast alloy, 5-stud fixing

Transmission			
	Front engine, rear transaxle connected by 20mm shaft in 4 bearings	Front engine, rear transaxle connected by 25mm shaft in 3 bearings	
Clutch	Single dry plate, 215mm diameter, cable operation	Single dry plate, 225mm diameter, hydraulic operation	
Gearbox	Audi 4-speed or 5-speed option (5-speed)	Porsche 5-speed	
Ratios			
1st		2.786	3.166
2nd		1.722	1.777
3rd		1.217	1.217
4th		0.931	0.931
5th		0.706	0.706
Final drive		4.714	4.125

Dimensions

Wheelbase	2,400mm (92.7in)	2,400mm (92.7in)
Front track	1,418mm (54.5in)	1,418mm (54.5in)
Rear track	1,372mm (53.0in)	1,392mm (53.8in)
Length	4,212mm (13ft 8in)	4,212mm (13ft 8in)
Width	1,685mm (65.2in)	1,685mm (65.2in)
Height	1,270mm (49.6in)	1,270mm (49.6in)

Capacities

Fuel tank	62 litres (13.6 gallons)	62 litres (13.6 gallons)
Engine oil	5 litres (8.8 pints)	5.5 litres (9.9 pints)
Coolant	7 litres (12.3 pints)	7 litres (12.3 pints)

Weights

DIN, dry	1,130kg (2,492lb)	1,180kg (2,612lb)

Performance

0–100km/h	9.6sec (5-speed)	7.8sec
Standing km	31.0sec	28.0sec
Top speed	125mph (200km/h)	140mph (225km/h)
DIN fuel consumption	36.8mpg	30.7mpg
at 56mph	42.8mpg	36.2mpg
at 75mph	34.9mpg	26.9mpg

The 924 Turbo's running gear shows some major differences. Apart from the entirely different induction system which involved a new cylinder head, the torque tube is 5mm thicker (25mm), the clutch is larger, and the Porsche five-speed gearbox is ahead of the differential, unlike the 924's Audi box, which is aft. The driveshafts are thicker, too.

Front three-quarter view of the 924 Turbo engine, which has a KKK turbocharger on the exhaust side of the engine and a long, cast-alloy tract crossing over to the induction. Special features included transistorized ignition, platinum-tipped spark plugs and a separate oil cooler. The engines were built and tested by Porsche technicians at Zuffenhausen.

About the only thing that people could criticize was the rather sudden onrush of power at 3,000rpm, which could be unsettling on slippery roads. It was all too reminiscent of the early 911 Turbo models, particularly those on Cinturato tyres before the P7 was introduced.

Everything else about the 924 Turbo was superb. It looked more purposeful, it sounded quieter and silkier (and at Weissach there was an experimental turbo engine with balancer-shafts, about which the engineers still enthuse). The brakes were virtually fade-free and the handling was just a little better, with Bilstein gas dampers on firmer settings, but

some customers were disappointed that Porsche hadn't done a bit more work on the cornering power, perhaps by lowering the suspension or fitting low-profile tyres. The engineers at Weissach are generally fairly conservative, though, and always kept durability and dependability as the main goals.

Right-hand drive cars for the British market were already a year behind due to the difficulty in converting the steering, the first arriving in Reading in November 1979 at a tax-paid retail price of £13,629. It was well-equipped, too, with a Panasonic stereo set, electric aerial, power windows, tinted glass all round, headlamp washers and a rear window wiper,

The polizei, of course, needed 924 Turbos on the autobahn fleet to keep up with the Schmidts.

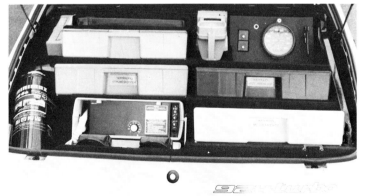

Well-equipped boot of the police version of the 924 Turbo, laden in a way that the 911's could never be.

and it soon acquired itself a waiting list.

In Stuttgart, though, there was concern about the 924 Turbo. Warranty claims were mounting up for turbo-related failures, what the engineers called 'the doctor syndrome'. The story is familiar enough to development engineers who work for any motor manufacturer in the world! 'The prototypes performed well in tests', Professor Bott recalls. 'The engine was troublefree when we tested it at high speeds, but the turbocharger gave trouble when the doctor visited his patients. It was not good for short journeys, heating up and cooling down.

'The KKK came from a truck, it was not designed for a car. A truck runs for a long time at constant speeds and loads, but this is not the case for all the cars we sell. We had a lot of

The turbo engine installed, in the first rhd car to reach Britain in November 1979. This, said the Porsche fans, was the car the 924 should always have been, with vivid performance (acceleration to 60mph in 7.7 seconds).

trouble developing the oil. We went through four or five different versions of the turbocharger and each one was better, but we did not really solve the problems until 1984 when the 944 Turbo was ready. Funnily enough we did not have problems with the 911 Turbo, because that is a large, powerful engine with low loads.'

As usual, though, marathon experts Rudi Lins and Gerhard Plattner experienced no technical difficulties in driving their new 924 Turbo from New York to Vienna, clocking up 37,000 kilometres (nearly 23,000 miles) through America, Africa and Europe in just 31 days. The run started at Fairbanks, Alaska, where the temperature was minus 60°C, pretty near to the cold record, and included an air-freight crossing from New York to Frankfurt before the crew headed south for the Sahara desert, returning to the northern climes of Sweden before the finish.

There were few changes for the 1980 model year (the first for UK and US deliveries). The emission-controlled US version developed 150bhp, a level that would be disappointing to European customers, but represented a tremendous bonus over the standard 924's 115bhp. A flap was designed to hide the fuel filler cap, and electric window lifters and a rear foglamp became standard equipment.

The 'second generation' 924 Turbo was announced in the summer of 1980 for the '81 model year, and despite Professor Bott's gloomy recollections, this car is one for the enthusiast even today. The compression ratio was raised to 8.5:1, a high figure for a turbo engine not equipped with an intercooler, and a smaller, faster-reacting KKK turbocharger was fitted.

Power went up from 170 to 177bhp, and there was a modest improvement in torque as well, rising from 180 to 184.5lb/ft at the same engine speed, 3,500rpm. The US version was also uprated with an 8.5:1 compression and the torque improved very slightly, from 152lb/ft to 155lb/ft. The power remained unchanged at 150bhp, but the real advantage, as with the European versions, was found in the

Endurance men Lins and Plattner gave the 924 Turbo a good welcome with a flat-out run at the Nardo proving ground in southern Italy. They averaged 130mph for 24 hours.

Garish interiors were back as the first rhd Turbos reached Reading. The smaller diameter steering wheel is leather-trimmed.

Fifteen-inch diameter wheels were specified for the 924 Turbo, still with 70-series tyres, although low-profiles were becoming popular with other manufacturers. A space-saver spare wheel was supplied, with an electric compressor connecting to the cigar lighter socket.

economy figures.

A key feature of the 1981 model 924 Turbo was the adoption of Digital Ignition Timing (DIT) developed jointly by Porsche, Siemens and Dr Hartig's Impuls-Technik company. This was the forerunner of the Motronic system developed by Bosch, and DIT made possible a far more accurate control of the ignition timing over a wide range of operating conditions. The system comprised a revs/reference point sensor adjacent to the flywheel, a temperature sensor in the inlet manifold, an electronic control unit containing a pressure sensor, and a throttle valve switch.

The DIT system had a profound effect on the fuel consumption, putting the 924 Turbo on a par with the 125bhp 924 model in the European standards. At a steady 56mph the consumption worked out at 42mpg, at 75mph it was 33mpg and in the urban cycle, 25mpg (Imperial figures). The overall improvement in consumption was to the order of 13%, and the car's range was extended considerably as the tank capacity was increased to 84 litres (18 gallons).

Government figures are all very well, but owners of Porsche

turbos tend not to drive them in the way that civil servants expect. An overall consumption figure better than 30mpg could be seen on a journey, especially at steady speeds on motorways, but use of the turbocharger's boost took its inevitable toll. Hard-driven journeys tended to raise the consumption to the range of 20–25mpg, still creditable for the amount of performance available.

The 0–60mph acceleration figure reduced to 7.5 seconds, 100mph could be reached in 17.5 seconds, and the maximum speed rose to 143mph (230km/h).

It's a great pity that Porsche's management swept the 924 Turbo out of the range to make way for the 944. Professor Bott makes it clear that problems in developing the turbocharger system weren't overcome, and suggests too that resources were put into the development of Porsche's own 2½-litre engine. Fair comment, but by comparison the 944 felt, well, bland when it was introduced, and many people thought it needed the extra 'go' of the turbo.

Although Porsche doesn't keep an exact record, it seems that 12,000 924 Turbos were made between 1978 and July

A smaller KKK turbocharger was fitted to the 1981 924 Turbos, and other changes included digital ignition timing (DZV in factory terminology), with the compression ratio raised to 8.5:1. Power went up to 177bhp, but the average improvement in fuel economy was 13%, and reliability was much better, too. This British market car is equipped with the optional 928S-style 'slab' wheels.

1982. Some 2,500 were made in the 1979 model year, 5,250 in the 1980 model year, when deliveries commenced to North America (3,440 sales) and the UK. Despite the improvements for the '81 model year, production tailed off to an estimated 3,000, then to around 1,300 in the final 12 months. The last batch of 924 Turbos made was earmarked for Italy, where a substantial tax-hike on cars over 2 litres threatened to give the 944 model a difficult debut.

924 gets the 'Carrera' label
Some people were prepared to be shocked when the hallowed 'Carrera' name was attached to a 924. The name, Spanish for 'race', had passed into Porsche mythology and conjured up recollections of the four-cam 356s, the type 550 and 718 competitions cars and, more recently, the most evocative 911 ever made.

Attachment of the Carrera label (nothing discreet, emblazoned in scarlet on the black paintwork) on a racey looking 924 at the Frankfurt Show in September 1979 meant one thing: the car was intended for racing. Sure enough,

Professor Fuhrmann had passed the word down, a team of three such cars would compete at Le Mans in June 1980.

Why? Everyone wanted the answer to that question. Most people in the company now knew that the Weissach engineers were progressing nicely with Porsche's own four-cylinder engine, and that a new model would be ready within three years. Why enter for the world's most famous sports car race with a 2-litre model that stood no chance of winning?

Why, asked the company's loyal supporters, run a four-cylinder production car at Le Mans when an outright winner occupied a corner at Weissach with a dust sheet thrown over it? Why, then, play down the 924 racing programme (the competitions model was designated 937) and propose to have the cars driven by factory employees, amateurs?

Perhaps the arguments hadn't been thought through properly. In England, John Aldington reacted quickly to the news and proposed that each of the three cars should have a nationality. PCGB would sponsor a 'British' entry for Tony Dron and Andy Rouse, first and second in the previous year's Porsche 924 Championship, and quite soon a positive

Photographed at Weissach prior to the 1979 Frankfurt Show, the 924 Carrera concept model transformed the deft lines of the normally aspirated car. Polyurethane was used for the front skirt, front wings and rear wheelarch flares, and a larger wing moulding was fitted to the back window.

The engineers (or stylists, maybe) were having difficulty in deciding whether to mount a snorkel air intake on the bonnet. When seen in public the appendage was in place, directing air to the intercooler, which was a direct benefit in raising the power to 210bhp.

Trouble was taken to clean up the airflow underneath the Carrera concept car, and aerodynamic efficiency was further increased by lowering it 10–15mm.

response came back from Zuffenhausen.

Later, PCGB would be asked to find a professional driver; John Watson priced himself out of the equation, which wasn't surprising, and Derek Bell asked for time to think it over (also not surprising, because he would have preferred another chance to win the race).

The episode turned out famously for everyone, as will be told in the next chapter. Juergen Barth and Manfred Schurti finished the 24-Hour race safely in sixth place overall, Dron and Rouse distinguished themselves on their debut at the circuit and Derek Bell raced the American car, driving for the first time with Al Holbert. Bell's career moved into high gear in June 1980, so he is among a number of people who should remember the 924 Carrera GT with affection.

The decision to launch the 924 Carrera GT was Professor Fuhrmann's and was in line with his philosophy, going back to his appointment in 1971, to compete with production or production-based cars. The 911 Turbo, the base for the 934 and 935 competitions models, was an example of how Prof Fuhrmann wanted the company to go about things, and he

intended history to repeat itself in 1980. Knowing that the 944 model would be along later, Fuhrmann aimed to give the car shape, and concept, the full Porsche treatment . . . when the 'proper' engine came along, it would be better still.

The 924 Carrera GT broke some new ground, and pointed the way to developments in the 1980s. Styling director Tony Lapine was responsible for the 'wide body' look with flared front and rear wheelarches, though very aware that the rear arches were literally, and evidently tacked-on in the last stages of assembly. The arches were made of fibre-reinforced polyurethane, the material used for the 928's flexible front and rear body panels, and would spring back into shape after an impact.

The front 'bumper' was incorporated into a deep air dam, also made of polyurethane, and was much more aerodynamic-looking; so too was the flexible rubber spoiler around the back window, with about twice the area of that on the 924 Turbo and sufficient even for racing.

It was a menacing looking machine in black or Guards red, the only colours offered. Fuchs forged-alloy wheels, 15 or 16

Many people consider the 924 Carrera GT to be the most aggressive four-cylinder model ever made by Porsche, spoiled in detail only by having the 'tacked on' flares for the rear arches. This model compared closely with the contemporary 3-litre 911 in both performance and price. Fifteen-inch Fuchs-style wheels were standard for the Carrera GT, with black centres and polished rims, with the 16in wheels from the 928S as an option. Brakes and suspension were the same as the 924 Turbo's.

Clearly based on the 924 Turbo model, the Carrera GT raised the 2-litre engine's power to 210bhp largely due to the intercooler, which lowered the temperature of the charged air by 50 degrees C.

Of the 406 Carrera GTs made, 200 were sold in Germany and 75 in Britain, where they were priced nominally at £19,000. Within days of the first deliveries, Carreras were advertised in the mid-twenties, the first 924 model to attract a premium.

inches in diameter, were straight from the top 911 model, with black centres and polished 7J rims. The optional 16-inch wheels were equipped with Pirelli P7 tyres, a popular choice. The Carrera GT retained the Turbo's four-slot nose panel, but this, now, was serving the intercooler that became part of the specification. The NACA duct on the bonnet was transformed into a full-scale air scoop standing proud of the sheet metal, and designed to catch the attention of every BMW driver who looked in his mirror. The brakes, suspension components, steering and gearbox were the same as in the 924 Turbo model, but the suspension was lowered by 10mm at the front and by 15mm at the rear.

The windscreen was bonded in, a novelty in the Porsche range, and those who complained that a passenger door mirror was an option were told that it cut the top speed by 2km/h! The Carrera's drag coefficient was kept to 0.34 despite the fitting of wide wheels, but the kerb weight was a little disappointing at 1,180kg (2,600lb). The intention to fit lightweight aluminium doors and bonnet, saving 150kg, was postponed for the GTS 'evolution' model that followed.

Already the 924 Turbo was the world's most powerful 2-litre car with 170bhp, so the Carrera GT was a real champion with 210bhp on offer. The intercooler lowered the temperature of the charged air by 50°C, and improved the combustion by some 15%. The compression was raised to 8.5:1 and the new Digital Ignition System was fitted for the first time. Production of the 406 Carrera GTs started in August 1980, at the same time as the first 177bhp 924 Turbo went down the line, and was completed by Christmas, so it couldn't be claimed that either model was 'first' with digital ignition!

When introduced to the British market in October 1980 the Carrera GT was priced at £19,000, about the same as a 911 and with similar performance. The price was rather academic, perhaps, since the 75 right-hand drive cars allocated to Britain were ordered well ahead, and the first ones changed hands at a substantial premium almost immediately. Two hundred were sold in the German domestic market, incidentally, at DM60,000 and the remaining 125 went to Austria, Switzerland, France, Italy

The black car retained by PCGB had a sombre-looking interior, but the 911 Sport seats were comfortable and offered excellent location. No road-testers were disappointed by this car, which had a top speed of 150mph.

and other European markets.

This was further proof, I believe, that the origin of the 2-litre engine was not a strong drawback to the success of the 924 model. The main criterion, always, was the performance level, with as much refinement as can be mustered (if Lotus fans can enthuse about a Japanese engine in the new Elan, surely anything goes nowadays?). The level of performance was, of course, stunning as the Carrera GT had a top speed of 150mph, and could reach 60mph from a standing start in 6.7 seconds, against 7.5 seconds for the second series 924 Turbo.

Here was a sports car that seemed to be packed with energy, ready to release an explosive charge of acceleration when asked. If anything the initial acceleration seemed stronger than the 911 Turbo's, thanks perhaps to the lower first gear ratio, but this was the Porsche transmission remember, and second gear wasn't guaranteed when shifting from first!

The Carrera GT seems likely to achieve something near classic status, but the ultimate was yet to come. In the first quarter of 1981 a total of 59 'evolution' cars was built, the GTS model with 245bhp in standard form, or 275bhp in club sport trim. These were followed by a total of 19 GTR models, which were virtually replicas of the 1980 Le Mans team cars, though with 375bhp.

Just as Porsche had lined up 25 type 917s for the FIA's

inspection in 1969, the company presented 50 identical 924 Carrera GTS models, all painted scarlet, outside the Zuffenhausen plant in March 1981. At higher boost, 1.0bar (14.1 pounds), the engines developed 245bhp at 6,250rpm, and 247lb/ft of torque at 3,000rpm, a particularly good figure for a competitions engine.

The Carrera GTS did benefit from the aluminium doors and engine cover made, originally, for the 1979 show car, and the weight came down to 1,121kg (2,472 pounds). The specification included coil springs at the rear, replacing the usual torsion bars, and cast aluminium rear suspension trailing arms instead of the steel fabricated arms that originated on the VW Beetle Cabriolet. Ventilated and cross-drilled brakes came straight from the 911 Turbo, and therefore differed little from those on the 935 model.

Performance was in keeping with the car's purpose in life as the 0–100km/h (62.1mph) time was reduced to 6.2 seconds, and the maximum speed went up to 250km/h (155mph). A 120-litre safety fuel tank was installed, and the price went up steeply to DM110,000, with export prices to be negotiated –

Derek Bell has one of these cars, assigned originally as part of his contract, and Richard Lloyd another.

Even higher road performance was offered by the club race or rally version with a 275bhp version of the same engine, maximum power achieved at 6,400rpm with a maximum torque figure of 270lb/ft at 3,600rpm. The price was higher still at DM145,000, but included underbody protection for the rally man, and suspension raised as required. For this version a maximum speed of 260km/h could be expected (161mph) with the 0–100km/h time cut to 5.9 seconds.

Ultimately, at DM180,000, the 924 Carrera GTR could be ordered by a customer and delivered ready for racing, with 375bhp available at a turn of the key. This was considerably more powerful than the car raced to sixth place at Le Mans, and part of the improvement was due to the Bosch-Kugelfischer plunger pump fuel injection system which hadn't been ready the previous June. A high-lift camshaft was included along with the dry-sump lubrication system, and the boost pressure was raised to the region of 1.4bar.

The GTR had none of the exotic materials of the works

When the Carrera GT run had been completed a further series of lightweight evolution cars was built in the first quarter of 1981. The GTS was available with a standard 245bhp, or with a club sport engine developing 275bhp, and the GTR rally or circuit cars were offered with up to 375bhp.

Still with the standard 1,984cc capacity, the 924 Carrera GTS engine was boosted at 1bar (14.1lb) and developed 245bhp. It required massive cooling for the water (the radiator was enlarged), the oil, and the charged air; the intercooler is above the cylinder head.

cars, titanium being the most obvious example, but it was otherwise a fair replica. It had the full 935 brake system including the special calipers, 11.75 x 16in BBS racing wheels with centre bolts, adjustable front and rear anti-roll bars, an extended rear spoiler, sintered metal clutch linings, and a locked differential.

The weight was quoted at 945kg, the minimum for the class, but Juergen Barth noted that the cars which raced at Le Mans in 1981 as private entries all weighed just over 1,000kg. Porsche even quoted performance figures for the GTR including a 0–100km/h time of 4.7 seconds, and a maximum speed of 290km/h (180mph).

Professor Fuhrmann left Porsche in December 1980 to lecture at the University of Vienna, and his successor, Peter

Schutz, had a very different style. His ambitions coincided with those of Professor Porsche, indeed they had talked at considerable length over a period of some months. The demise of the 911, planned for 1984, was cancelled and the six-cylinder-powered 936 was reintroduced to uphold the company's prestige at Le Mans.

The 944 was raced in prototype form at Le Mans in 1981, and once the last 924 Carrera GTR had been built and delivered in the summer of that year the Weissach engineers consigned it to history. All future development would concentrate upon the 944, 911 and 928 road cars, and the new Group C 956 racing car, every one of these, of course, powered by an engine designed and built by Porsche.

CHAPTER 3

Enter the 944

New engine for a new model

A euphoric welcome awaited the Porsche 944 when it reached the world markets. After the announcement in June 1981, shortly after the successful debut run at Le Mans, another six months passed by before the car went on sale in Germany, and other European markets followed in the first half of 1982. When it went on sale in Britain in May the order book accounted for two years of imports, and there was a ready demand in America, too, where the 944 had been on sale since April. Straight away, it would become the fastest-selling Porsche ever produced.

Much of the technology already existed. The body was largely that of the 924 model, though with distinctively flared wheelarches; the platform was that of the 924 Turbo in respect of the hubs, ventilated brake discs, suspensions and the 25mm torque tube in three bearings; the gearbox was a five-speed from Audi, suitably strengthened, or a VW-sourced three-speed automatic. The steering now came from ZF, and power assistance, when it became available a year later as an option, was speed-variable like that on the 928, and extremely unobtrusive.

There had been a considerable debate at Porsche before the decision was made to develop a unique four-cylinder engine. Six and eight-cylinder engines were examined, and a prototype existed with the 'PRV' Euro V6, but nobody liked it very much because it was coarse and lacked power. Personally, Professor Bott liked the 924 Turbo engine equipped, experimentally, with twin counter-balance shafts, a design invented by Frederick Lanchester early in the century and patented, much later on, by Mitsubishi.

'It was clearly the way to go, especially with the higher capacities we had in mind', Bott explains. 'We wanted an engine that we could develop in three or four stages, as we had with the 911, always finding more power. We wanted it to be economical to make, and easy to service.

'Especially we did not want to have three engine families in our range. We counted the 911 and the 911 Turbo as one family, with six cylinders; we counted the 928 as another, and we wanted the 944 to be of the same family. It has the same cylinder head, in principle, the same bore sizes and spacings, the same valves, and the same steering system. In fact, it is not known that the 944 four-valve engine, the 928S4 and the 959 model all have the same valves, valve guides, valve angles, and even the same combustion chamber; even the same steering parts. When you find the optimum, naturally you apply it to every type of engine where possible.'

The V6 and V8 engines that some people wanted would clearly start a new family tree at Weissach, something the company could not afford, and didn't want to contemplate. Jochen Freund adds another dimension: 'At the time, in 1979, the world was still very conscious of energy conservation. We wanted the best fuel economy and for many reasons a four-cylinder is the best proposition. Anyway, we wanted the engine to fit the existing chassis. Professor Fuhrmann said we must build a four, and most of us agreed with his decision.'

Porsche's 'four' was quite unlike any other that existed. It was introduced at nearly 2½-litres capacity and could be taken to just over 3 litres. It was, straight away, at the upper

Porsche's 'wide body' theme was developed for the 944 model announced in 1981 and produced from early '82. It had been intended to place the balancer-shaft engine into the 924's narrow body, but incoming chairman Peter Schutz had a better idea.

end of the range for an in-line four-cylinder unit, especially one constructed almost entirely in aluminium alloys.

The twin, contra-rotating balancer shafts were the key to smooth performance, one positioned underneath the inlet manifold and the other lower down on the other side of the block, below the exhaust manifold. They were driven at twice the crankshaft speed by means of a cogged belt (a separate belt was used for the water pump and camshaft, and a third drove the alternator). Tests showed that the balancer shaft system absorbed three or four horsepower at maximum engine speed, an entirely acceptable figure for an engine so efficient otherwise.

With counter-balance shafts the engine became 'completely different' says Prof Bott. 'It was so smooth. In the beginning we were a little concerned because we checked the Mitsubishi engine and it wasn't very good. In fact, even with balancer shafts it had more vibration than our 944 engine without them! We were very sensitive to criticisms about noise and harshness, because these were the main complaints about the 924, especially at higher rpm.'

The 944 engine closely resembled one bank of the 928's V8, and the identical 100mm bore dimension produced the 122mm bore centre spacing and allowed the same pistons to be used. The cylinder block used the 'open deck' design

The first 944s to be delivered in the British market made many customers happy in May 1982. They marvelled at the silky smoothness of the balancer-shaft four-cylinder engine, which was reminiscent of a 'six' or even an 'eight'.

without liners, and using the Reynolds Aluminium technique pioneered by Chevrolet (first on the McLaren CanAm cars) the piston skirts were sprayed with iron so that they'd run smoothly in the aluminium bores.

The crankcase extended downwards to the centreline of the main bearings, and extra rigidity came from the use of a one-piece 'ladder' casting incorporating all the main bearing caps. The aluminium sump contributed to the strength of the engine, too, and was heavily baffled. The forged steel crankshaft ran in five main bearings and looked massive – it was designed to accommodate double the standard power output – and the pistons were propelled by sintered steel connecting rods.

As for the cylinder head itself, it was almost the same as the 928's except for a small modification to the two-valve combustion chamber shape. It featured hydraulic tappets which were incorporated into the inverted buckets, doing away with the need for rockers. The entire camshaft assembly was a separate unit, complete with its own oil gallery, bolting onto the cylinder head for easy installation and maintenance.

Porsche's TOP research was used to the full in the design of the head and combustion chamber as a high compression ratio of 10.6:1 was used. The spark plug was offset so that a wedge-shaped combustion chamber could be developed, with a strong squish effect. Bosch L-Jetronic injection was installed along with digital electronic ignition, a forerunner of the fully mapped Motronic system.

The engine's maximum output of 163bhp (or more roundly, 120kW) was achieved at relatively modest revs, 5,800rpm, and represented an increase of 30% compared with the 2-litre 924 model. Even more impressive, though, was the torque value, a 'curve' that was practically flat and exceeded 140lb/ft between 2,000rpm and 6,000rpm. The parabola peaked at 151lb/ft at 3,000rpm, and the engine's performance across the range was widely admired. It was also notably economical on fuel and *Autocar*'s test routine included an overall figure of 26.2mpg (10.8 litres per 100kms), or 28.8mpg excluding the performance tests. The government tests produced an urban consumption of 25.2mpg, and 30.1mpg at a steady 70mph.

The 944 engine is made almost entirely of light alloys and is, in effect, one-half of Porsche's V8. When Dr Lanchester's balancer-shaft invention was applied to a 924 Turbo engine in 1978 it was apparent immediately that this was the way to go, and all experience has been favourable.

hydraulic dampers which served as the main mounting points onto a new type of aluminium chassis crossmember. These were likened by Jochen Freund to the dampers inside a washing machine, and were developed specifically to overcome a weakness noted on the US-market 924s.

The 924's engine mounts had a pretty short life due to what the engineers termed 'freeway hop', the constant 'der-dum . . . der-dum' over the bitumen seals at 55mph (or

There were two unusual features about the ancillaries. Porsche's design team pioneered the use of an oil/water intercooler attached to the engine block, and surrounded by coolant. Warm-up of the oil was speeded by its proximity to coolant, and at high speeds the temperature of the oil was kept down very efficiently by the same means.

The engine was inclined at an angle of 30-degrees to vertical so as to fit the existing bay, and was located by two

A cutaway 944 was prepared for the 1981 Frankfurt Show, revealing all. With Bosch Motronic engine management the four-cylinder unit developed 163bhp; underneath, the suspension and brake systems were developed from the 924 Turbo.

MacPherson struts have served the 924/944 models well, the gas-filled dampers having been uprated at intervals. The engine is mounted on two small hydraulic dampers which insulate noise and vibration.

Porsche's fully galvanized bodies have a 10-year corrosion warranty (against perforations), the best in the motor industry. The boot floor could be lower, say the engineers, but for the size of Audi's transmissions.

more). Even though these special mounts were troublesome at first they were copied by a number of other manufacturers, notable Mercedes and Audi, and they certainly contribute to the 944's level of comfort which is now taken for granted.

The 944 model was introduced in Germany with a surprisingly low price tag of DM38,900, and reached Britain at a tax-paid price of £13,000. Power steering wasn't available for another year, though it was quickly incorporated into the standard specification, and generally the new model was at least 15% less expensive than the worldwide dealer network had anticipated. Finance director Heinz Branitzki worked out a comfortable sales price of DM42,000 for the 944, but Peter Schutz wanted to run an introductory offer price of DM35,000, cutting margins right to the bone, and sales director Lars-Roger Schmidt became involved in a lively crossfire until the compromise price tag was agreed.

In a way the seeds were sown for major difficulties later on, as the price of the 944 Turbo had to be kept artificially low, below that of the 911, when it was launched in 1985. 'While the dollar was strong the company could stand it', explains

944 dashboard was originally similar to that of the 924, though with detail differences and a restyled steering wheel.

Seen for the first time at the Stockholm Show in February 1985, and incorporated almost immediately, was the all-new Porsche-designed dashboard for the 944 model. It featured 928-style instruments in a stylishly curved facia, and was designed for air-bag application in the US models.

The 1986 944 (produced from September 1985) benefited from a number of Turbo model features. These included the cast aluminium suspension arms front and rear, greater sump capacity and oil flow, a larger (80-litre) fuel tank, and the battery moved to the rear. 'Telephone dial' wheels were adopted.

Schmidt, 'but when the dollar went down it made big problems.'

Porsche themselves claimed that the balancer-shaft four-cylinder engine was as smooth as a six, and no-one disagreed when the chance came to drive the 944. Some, in fact, thought it to be as good as an 'eight'. So smooth was the engine in operation that it no longer mattered how many cylinders it had, and few would have guessed it was a 'four' without looking under the bonnet. The disadvantage, and it was real enough, was a psychological one: the owner of a 944 would never throw open the bonnet with pride, as would the owner of a 928. He'd show what it could do out there on the road, not in the golf club car park.

Although there weren't very many owners of 924 Turbos in the world, the new 944 wasn't a car that would appeal to them. It lacked not only 14 horsepower but any form of characteristic 'punch', due of course to the wide spread of torque. The weights of the two cars were almost identical: Porsche claimed 1,180kg for both and *Autocar* weighed the 944 and found it to be just 34lb (15.4kg) heavier.

'Porsche set out to produce a large four-cylinder engine with close to six-cylinder levels of smoothness and refinement' *Autocar*'s test team reported. 'They have not only succeeded in that aim, but have also produced perhaps the most relaxed and effective power unit of this size we have met in recent years . . . this new Porsche engine is both very flexible and untemperamental. It has the kind of power curve that forgives a forgotten downchange when overtaking, or the gear shift being left in second when restarting. What it lacks in sheer power it gains in its wonderfully effective spread of torque.'

Excellent fuel economy, superb handling (better than the 924's thanks to suspension improvements and wider wheels) and fine brakes were strong plus-points. The magazine was mildly critical of road noise coming into the cabin – always a criticism of the 924 – the negative-offset front suspension geometry following the contours of the road, the VW-inspired dashboard, and over-sensitive brake pedal response. 'It is superbly finished and has a unique balance of qualities that for the price make the few niggles utterly insignificant.'

After reducing the power for one year to 160bhp, Porsche raised it again for the 1989 model year to 165bhp (121kW) when the capacity was increased to 2,681cc. This proved to be the last production year of the eight-valve, normally aspirated 944. In future the company would concentrate on the Turbo and the 16-valve 'S' version.

The 944's quoted maximum speed of 220km/h was matched exactly by *Autocar*'s 137mph, while the claimed 0–100km/h time of 8.4sec was certainly bettered by a 0–60mph time of 7.4sec. The 0–100mph time, always the most interesting for a very high performance car, just missed greatness at 21.0 seconds, but we were still in early days.

Not surprisingly, the three-speed automatic version was rather less lively, with a claimed 9.6sec from rest to 100km/h (62.1mph) and 25sec to 100mph. More to the point, though, it was substantially quicker than even the manual 924, and now offered a very acceptable level of performance to those who didn't want responsibility for a five-speed manual box.

It hadn't been so important to Porsche for a new model to be well accepted since the 911 was launched in 1964. The 911 was a 'make or break' replacing the 356, the model upon which the company's fame and fortune had been built, and the introductions of the 924 (1976) and 928 (1978) have been useful rather than vital.

The 944, though, was another matter. Professor Fuhrmann had, until his sudden departure in December 1980, intended the turbocharged version which followed to replace the 911. Professor Ferry Porsche was having none of this, and early in 1981 Peter W. Schutz made it his first task to confirm that the 911 was timeless and irreplaceable. The announcement of the 944 was only a few months away (a desperately short timespan for the incorporation of the flared wheelarches, intended for the turbo model three years hence), and although the 944 wasn't the first component in the company's future, it was still a main element.

Peter Schutz, Professor Bott and other board members carried out a heavy-hitting campaign in the States 'We had eight or ten questions which we put to 45 people in the American organization', recalls Prof Bott. 'They were people like dealer principals, sales and service managers. I drove with these people myself, and asked the questions personally. "Is this car, in your eyes, a real Porsche or not?" And 45 times I got the answer "Yes". It did not matter how many cylinders it had, so long as it did the job well. They said they could sell the car in high numbers, and we went away happy.'

In 1983, the first full calendar year of sales in America, the

This is the US-specification 944 for 1989, distinguished externally from the European-market car by alloy wheels in the flat style first seen on the 928S, side marker lights and door rubbing strip.

VW-owned Audi Porsche organization sold 13,700 of the 944s; in 1984 the figure dropped a little to 12,883 on account of the German metalworkers' strike, but 1985 broke all records at 15,459 US sales, the best for any Porsche model.

Half-way through the year, at the start of the 1984 model year in fact, power steering was offered as an option (but, for the British market, was standard equipment with automatic transmission). The system was virtually identical to that of the 928 model with the level of power assist depending on engine speed; at parking speed there was maximum assistance, diminishing at higher speed. With the steering rack ratio increased from 22:1 to 18.5:1 (lower numerically, but with a greater turning moment) the system immediately became extremely popular, and was incorporated as standard equipment 12 months later.

Power steering was particularly useful when the optional forged alloy wheels were fitted, 16in diameter and with 7J/8J rims front and rear. A Sport suspension pack was offered with heavier anti-roll bars and uprated gas dampers, and at long last an electrically operated catch released the rear hatch window from inside the car. The sunroof, if ordered as an option, had an electric tilt mechanism at the back. It was never possible to slide the sunroof back in the normal way, though, simply because the roof area wasn't large enough.

The German metalworkers' union staged a five-week strike in the spring of 1984 – intelligently they centered it on Stuttgart so as to damage Mercedes, Robert Bosch and Porsche, and soon Europe's motor industry as the supply of electrical components dwindled! This cost Porsche an estimated 5,660 cars valued at DM270 million, and was the principal reason why the start of the 1985 model year was delayed until October. Also affected was the announcement of the 944 Turbo, delayed until February 1985 and described in the next chapter.

One of the features of the Turbo model, shared by the 944 Lux, was the new-shaped dashboard. Stylishly sculpted with a gentle curve falling away to the centre of the console, the instrument panel was an immediate success. The old-style, original dashboard was retained for the 924 model in its final year, and even for the 2½-litre 924S, but at last the interior of

Again the Polizei were good customers of Porsche, buying the 944 for autobahn patrols.

Not sure if that's Gerhard Plattner, the Austrian Porsche PR man, inside the suit, but he visited Cape Canaveral in the course of his 500,000-kilometre drive in 1987. The object of Operation Luna 944 was to drive as far as the the moon and back within 12 months.

Back at Weissach, Professor Ferry Porsche signs his name on the car watched by Herr Plattner. To the right of Professor Porsche in the photo are Professor Helmuth Bott, head of research and development, PR man Uwe Brodbeck and sales director Hans Halbach.

The distinctive signature of Professor Porsche.

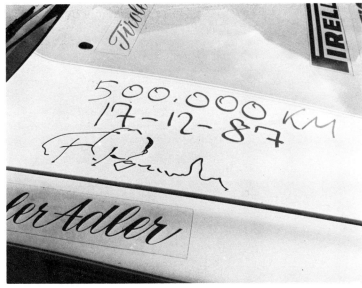

the 944 became different visually.

Heated windscreen washer nozzles, and the option of a graduated tint for the windscreen, were all that Porsche could announce for the 1985 model year 944, but at the Stockholm Show in February 1985 the new dashboard was seen for the first time. The design included a height-adjustable steering wheel, something else that customers for four-cylinder cars had wanted since 1976, and the throughflow of air from the facia vents was increased by 35%.

The 944 model now accounted for slightly more than half of Porsche's sales, a total of 50,514 worldwide in the 1985 model year, rising to 53,625 in the 1986 model year. Peter Schutz's expansionist policies were paying massive dividends as profits peaked at DM120.4 million in 1985, and a sum two-and-a-half times as big was invested in the start of Works V, which will accommodate the production of four-cylinder Porsches from January '91, and in new facilities at Weissach including a full-size wind-tunnel.

Porsche's marketing department went into top gear as the 1986 model year range was announced. In the four-cylinder family the 944 Turbo was clearly established as the flagship model, the 944 shared the benefit of many improvements, and the 2-litre 924 was finally replaced by the 2½-litre 924S.

The 944's power rating remained at 163bhp while the 924S was introduced at 150bhp, but a great many things were changed. In the suspension department, the fabricated front wishbones and rear trailing arms were replaced by cast aluminium components designed for the turbo model. 'The rear suspensions came from the Volkswagen Beetle Cabriolet, and we were the only people still using them', recalls Ing Freud. 'They could make enough for us in less than a week.' The last VW-originated components had been dispensed with, but specialized components cost money and Porsche prices were on the upward march.

Sump capacity was increased from 5.5 to 6.0 litres, with a stronger pump and larger oil galleries allowing the flow to be increased by 10%. This wasn't only to do with the needs of the turbo version, because there had been some worrying claims for damaged engines resulting from the owners allowing the oil to fall below the recommended level. Whatever its virtues, Porsche's four-cylinder didn't like to be neglected in this way, and the '86 model modification made it a little more tolerant.

A number of other features were shared with the Turbo model: the transaxle was attached to the body at three points instead of four to reduce the level of noise transmitted; the battery was moved from the engine bay to the boot to bias the weight distribution rearwards; a moulded plastic fuel tank was installed with a capacity of 80 litres (this replaced the notion of creating more space in the rear); the fuse box and relays were moved from the passenger footwell to the bulkhead; the starter motor was redesigned to be quieter and lighter; the alternator capacity was increased to 115 amps; the seats were mounted 30mm lower, and could be heated, or height-adjusted electrically, as options; the automatic version showed the gear selected in the rev-counter, as on the 928; the Sekuriflex laminated screen was flush-bonded into place and incorporated the radio aerial; and finally, something the British importers had wanted for 30 years, the pivots for the windscreen wipers were moved to clear the screen more effectively, and the blades parked on the left.

Moving on 12 months to the 1987 model year (starting September 1986), ABS braking was introduced as an option across the range, with minor suspension modifications to suit. Also available optionally were Sport suspension packages developed in the Turbo Cup series consisting of stiffer springs, firmer damper settings and heavier anti-roll bars. The wheel bearings were strengthened, and the brake servo action was made more powerful.

Although 163bhp (120kW) was the power figure quoted most often, American customers and an increasing number of Germans and Swiss were pegged to 150bhp in the cars with emission controls. There were mixed feelings, clearly, in the summer of 1987 (1988 model year) when Porsche announced that the output of the 924S would be *raised* to 160bhp and that of the 944 would be *reduced* to the same figure.

However, 160bhp was the *world* output, the same for all markets. Those with emission controls would cheer, while Britain, France, Italy and other countries not yet to embrace catalyzers were advised that performance figures were not impaired. Nobody would notice the loss of 3bhp, but psychologically it wasn't a very good move. If high performance was important to the customer he could order the 16-valve 944S, a model already well established.

All this became academic to Peter Schutz when his contract was terminated in December 1987, nearly a year ahead of time. Sales were plummeting in America, due largely but obviously not entirely to the weakening dollar and the four-cylinder models bore the brunt: from 16,511 cars in the 1986 calendar year (944, S and Turbo combined), the figure dropped to 10,800 in the 1987 calendar year, to 6,146 in the whole of 1988 and to just 2,930 in 1989.

Heinz Branitzki, finance director and deputy chairman since 1972, stepped into the limelight on his appointment as chairman in January 1988, and his mission was to batten down the hatches, as hard as they'd go. Sales of the four-cylinder models were holding up well in other parts of the world, and the 911 and 928 lines were hardly affected at all. In his business report for 1987/88 Herr Branitzki told shareholders that turnover on vehicle sales fell from DM2,993 million to DM2,083 million, due almost entirely

Elegant views of the Porsche 944 Cabriolet 'Studie' shown at Frankfurt in 1985. Styled by Anatole Lapine, the prototype was built by Bauer, who hoped for a contract. Powered by Porsche's first 16-valve four-cylinder engine which developed 185bhp, it was, effectively, the forerunner of the 944S model. At Frankfurt there were at least three imitators in the specialist hall, but none as good as the authentic cabrio.

When is a Porsche not a Porsche? This PEP (Porsche Experimental Prototype) caused a great stir when pictures leaked into the press in 1987. In fact it's a mobile test bed in which four, six or eight cylinder engines can be located at the front, centre or rear! It could be used equally well for confidential research for clients.

to losses in the States. Vehicle production fell by 18,614, to just 31,362, but of these 14,270 were 'lost' sales of four-cylinder cars built at Neckarsulm and 4,344 were 'lost' from the six- and eight-cylinder production lines at Zuffenhausen.

No longer would Porsche strive for volume, and 30–35,000 cars per annum would be a comfortable ceiling in future. Despite these terrible results, a profit of DM25.3 million was recorded.

Looking back, Prof Bott is certain that the 944 model was not developed as it should have been, and that the Turbo and 16-valve variants became too expensive. 'I think that there are special rules for America, which account for the continuing popularity of the 911 and the swings of the four-cylinder cars. If you make a car like everyone else you lose the market, but if you make something really special, even in low numbers, you can hold your place.' There, it seems, is the key to four-cylinder model development: put as much distance as possible between Porsche and the Japanese challengers.

There was one more step for the normally aspirated, two-valve 944 to take, and for the 1989 model year it was produced in 2.7-litre form. This was a 'one-shot' development because after one year of production the two-valve was discontinued, and the four-cylinder range was simplified with just the four-valve 944S and Turbo model, the former in Cabriolet form.

The bore size was increased from 100mm to 104mm, the stroke remaining at 78.9mm, and the capacity rose to 2,681cc. The compression ratio was up, too, from 10.2:1 (this figure set the previous year, when the power was reduced to 160bhp) to an extremely high figure of 10.9:1. Even so, the engine was designed to run with emission controls and lead-free fuel, and the power went up by just 3% to 165bhp. Much more significant was the increase in torque, by a sizeable 8%. Still with a very broad band, the torque rose from 152lb/ft at 4,500rpm to 166lb/ft at 4,200rpm.

Contributing to these gains were larger inlet valves, new camshaft profiles with modified valve timing, and revised engine management. Now, ABS braking was extended to all Porsche models as standard equipment.

Although the factory claimed a time of 8.2 seconds for the 0–100km/h acceleration – say, 8.0 seconds for 0–60mph – *Autocar & Motor* comfortably reduced this to 7.0 seconds, while the 0–100mph figure was established at 20.0 seconds. The recorded maximum speed was down to 135mph, but the testers generously conceded that tyre scrub at Millbrook accounted for at least 5mph, so there was no reluctance to confirm the claimed 137mph.

Excellent figures indeed for a car that now weighed 1,290kg (or 1,320kg as tested by the British weekly magazine, with 47% on the front and 53% on the rear), but the overall fuel consumption figure had increased to 20.7mpg, and the UK tax-paid price had risen to £26,000.

The 924S model was discontinued at the end of the '88 model year so the 2.7-litre 944 became Porsche's 'entry level' model. In Britain the price had doubled in six years, which was rather more than the increase in the retail price index, but the level of comfort and equipment had risen too. The long-awaited Cabriolet body was reserved for the 944S model, not the 2.7, which was destined for its pension in the summer of 1989. Out, then, went the Audi three-speed automatic transmission from the range, since it wasn't beefy enough to cope with the 3-litre 944S power. At Weissach, though, there are plans to reintroduce an automatic, along the lines of the Tiptronic ZF/Porsche/Bosch development for the 911 Carrera 2 model launched in 1989.

CHAPTER 4

The 944 Turbo and 944S

Further technical excellence

More by accident than design, Porsche didn't have a stunningly fast four-cylinder car available between the summer of 1982, when the 924 Turbo went out of production, and February 1985, when the 944 Turbo was announced. Demand for the 924 and, particularly, the 163bhp 944 model was so overwhelmingly strong that no harm was done so far as the marketing department was concerned, but the engineers at Weissach understood, clearly, the demand from certain customers for a very high-performance version. In a way the engineers had already created the demand – didn't the '924 Prototype' that ran at Le Mans in June 1981 have a four-valve cylinder head and a turbocharger?

But for the metalworkers' strike in the spring of 1984, the Turbo model would certainly have been launched in the summer. The loss of five weeks of production meant a further period of disruption, so the start of the 1985 model year was pushed back to October, and the launch of the 944 Turbo to February. It was a great pity because a prototype Turbo model romped to an overwhelming victory in the Nelson Ledges 24-hour race in Ohio in July, but except for a press release the factory couldn't capitalize on the success.

The new model was certainly worth waiting for, of course. With the KKK turbocharger installed and a complete range of revisions, the power went up by 35% to 220bhp. The particular significance of this engine, though, was that it was Porsche's first 'world' engine, developing the same 220bhp with full three-way lambda probe emission controls , and this was nearly 50% more than the Americans had experienced

before. As for the torque, this increased massively compared with the 944, from 151lb/ft at 3,000rpm to a maximum of 243lb/ft at 3,500rpm, again with an incredibly wide spread. No more could people say that a turbocharged Porsche had sudden characteristics, or was in any way difficult or tricky in adverse conditions.

Peter Schutz was understandably a proud man when he introduced the 150mph Porsche 944 Turbo to European and American journalists at St Paul de Vence in southern France in February 1985. No longer, he said, would the Americans be second-class citizens. No longer would the Americans be kept waiting for lower-powered versions. All of Porsche's new models would develop the same power worldwide. He also explained that this would force the grey market to contract, this being a market in America for new and secondhand European cars with higher power levels.

A third factor, less emphasized, was that US-standard emission controls were within sight in Switzerland, Austria and Germany itself, and Porsche's customers were going to expect, even demand, superior performance despite the fitment of catalytic converters.

Technically, the most significant feature of the new model was the use of the KKK company's K26 turbocharger, a new design with a water-cooled bearing housing and a thermally decoupling turbine wheel. By installing the turbocharger on the left side of the engine, that is on the opposite side to the exhaust, the gas entry temperature was reduced by about 90-degrees C, and the flow of normal coolant water around the turbine housing kept temperatures down to 170-degrees C

72

Cutaway view of the high-performing Porsche 944 Turbo model, announced in February 1985 and put into production in July. The power output was 220bhp for all world markets, even with a catalytic converter installed.

even at full load.

After the engine was switched off the water flow was maintained for a while by a thermic-syphon circuit, boosted by a thermostat-controlled water pump if necessary. Now, powertrain development manager Dipl Ing Paul Hensler was able to announce, oil carbonization did not occur; damage to bearings and seals was avoided, and the life of the turbocharger was considerably improved. The unique oil-water heat exchanger featured on the normal 944 was replaced by an external oil cooler, served by a separate intake in the nose and regulated by a thermostat in the same way as in the coolant system.

Of course, the 944 Turbo had an air-to-air intercooler like the 924 Carrera GT (a model built five years previously, but with 210bhp from 2.0 litres), and it reduced the temperature of inducted air by up to 75-degrees C.

Since the Carrera GT was produced the electronics had advanced dramatically. The Bosch engine management system, now the full Motronic, was so sophisticated that it controlled the turbocharger's wastegate as well, the opening of which was dependent not only on boost pressure but on approach to the knock limit, measured by a probe between the second and third cylinders, after 256 ignition pulses. In the case of overloading, the ignition would be retarded by

The 944 Turbo's five-speed gearbox is sourced from Audi, though substantially strengthened. It is located behind the differential. Suspension arms were cast in aluminium alloy for the first time.

three to six degrees with a noticeable reduction in performance, and if that wasn't enough the boost pressure would be reduced. If, on the other hand, the driver needed more power for acceleration, the turbocharger's wastegate would remain closed briefly while the throttle was fully opened, allowing up to 10% more torque.

Forged pistons replaced cast aluminium, and in the cylinder head ceramic liners were cast into the exhaust ports, raising the gas temperature by 30-degrees C, benefiting both the turbocharger's response and the efficiency of the catalysts. The inlet valves were made of new materials capable of withstanding higher thermal loadings, and the

exhaust valves had Nimonic heads and sodium-filled stems. A new oil pump increased the flow by about 10%, and the flow characteristics were improved in a modified engine block.

With typical thoroughness, the entire car was upgraded to suit the higher performance. The clutch was increased to 240mm diameter, and asbestos-free materials were used for the plates; an over-centre spring was incorporated to reduce pedal pressure. The five-speed gearbox came from Audi as usual (no automatic was available) but it had a stronger crownwheel and pinion, wider gear wheels and larger bearings, as well as special materials and craftsman assembly. All five ratios were altered to maximize the acceleration, but

Graceful lines of the 944 Turbo, in flight. Professor Fuhrmann's plan had been for the Turbo model, due a year earlier, to replace the 911, and to be the first 'wide-bodied' four-cylinder model. Two wide slats were incorporated in the air dam, instead of one for the normally aspirated 944. Above the number-plate is a separate opening to duct air to the intercooler.

The study of air flow underneath the body was pursued for the 944 Turbo, which featured a diffuser at the rear, extracting the air faster. Wide-section tyres, Pirelli P7s in this early picture, were needed to put 220bhp down effectively. Negative-offset wheels and suspension layout were needed as ABS braking was initially an option, becoming a standard feature in the 1987 model year.

fifth was shortened since, as Herr Hensler said, overdrive characteristics are not logical for cars with such high maximum speeds.

The drivetrain was attached to the chassis at three main points instead of four to reduce the interior noise/vibration levels, and the 60-litre steel fuel tank was replaced by an 80-litre tank made of polyethylene, a material easier to shape for the space available, and a closed-loop venting system was adopted to reduce emissions.

Aluminium castings replaced fabricated steel suspension arms, both at the front and the rear, finally doing away with the last VW components. The 944's floating-caliper brakes were replaced by Porsche-developed four-piston fixed calipers made of lightweight, heat-resistant aluminium alloy, still working on large-diameter ventilated discs (298mm diameter, 28mm thick at the front and 24mm thick at the rear). Again, asbestos-free pad materials were specified.

Cast aluminium wheels, 7J x 16 front and 8J x 16 rear, were standard equipment with 205/55 and 225/50 tyres, but as an option the car could be ordered with the familiar Fuchs forged alloy wheels, in the same sizes. Twin-tube pressurized gas dampers were installed instead of twin-tube fluid dampers, with the suspension firmed-up.

The 944 Turbo was distinguished by the polyurethane nose fairing incorporating the orange turn signals in wide housings above the passing lights, and two horizontal slits in the air dam took care of most of the cooling needs. Even the underside was airflowed with a rudimentary ground-effect system, and a rear under-spoiler helped to raise the downforce on the back wheels, remove heat and reduce vulnerability to side-winds.

The windscreen was now flush-bonded (and incorporated the radio antenna) and the drag coefficient was reduced from 0.35 to 0.33 (as mentioned before, an excellent figure for a car with such wide wheels). With a frontal area of 1.89sq m, the 944 Turbo had a Cd x F value of 0.624, the best of any production car in the world.

Porsche's new curved dashboard, featuring clear 928-style instruments, was introduced on the Turbo model, but incorporated on the 944 as well, and offered vertical adjustment of the steering wheel. The 911's new seating was installed, with electric adjustment, the electrical and fuse system was upgraded, and the air conditioning system redesigned for better service.

The introduction in southern France was an unqualified success because none of the journalists could remember a more docile, tractable turbocharged car. Boosted power didn't arrive with a rush, but in a well-controlled manner from 2,500rpm upwards. More than ever the four-cylinder engine felt like a 5-litre V8, for example, and gave the 944 giant-sized performance. Calibrated tests would soon confirm that the 944 Turbo could accelerate from rest to 60mph in 5.9 seconds (*Motor* test) and to 100mph in 14.9 seconds.

Early in 1988 a series of 1,000 Porsche 944 Turbos was made with the 250bhp Turbo Cup-specification engine. So successful was it that the uprated unit was put into series production for the 1989 model year.

Along with the more powerful engine, the '89-series 944 Turbo, seen here in US specification, had a heavier (1.25in diameter) front anti-roll bar, heavier springs and uprated rear torsion bars.

My yardstick of a high-performance car is that it should be capable of reaching 100mph in under 20 seconds, and in 1985 anything that could reach 'the ton' in under 15 seconds was nearing supercar status. Five years later, the model would need to break 12 seconds to be regarded as a supercar!

More than that, the Turbo's power kept going . . . the 100–120mph acceleration figure proved that, 8.5 seconds against 9.1 seconds for a contemporary 911 Carrera (*Fast Lane*). This, it will be remembered, was the model that Prof Fuhrmann intended to replace the 911, against the wishes of Prof Porsche, and it was quite clear that while the 944 Turbo could match the six-cylinder car in performance, its appeal was utterly different.

It made no great demands on the driver, it was quiet and sophisticated, outstanding though conventional in layout and handling. In short, a devoted 911 man would label the 944 Turbo cissy, and wouldn't be sorry to hand it back after a trial. The 944 Turbo customer, on the other hand, would be from a different generation and wouldn't be able to understand the 911's raw appeal (I should clarify here that

the modern Carrera 2 and Carrera 4 models are themselves much more sophisticated, and easier to handle, than their illustrious forebears).

As standard equipment the 944 Turbo had excellent power steering, like that on the 928S model, and ABS braking was available optionally. In 1986, a small number of cars were prepared for sale to racing teams for the Porsche Turbo Cup series, a spectacular set of races which confirmed the technical merit of the new model and gave it a competitions image that, so far, the 944 had lacked. The engines were strictly limited to the standard 220bhp and raced with catalytic converters installed.

Production of the 944 Turbo began in May 1985 and it went on sale in Germany at DM72,500, just DM500 more than the 911 Carrera; it went on sale in Britain in October priced at £25,311, but the price included £1,200 worth of air conditioning as standard equipment. All markets benefited from the Porsche factory's exceptional warranty terms which included a two-year guarantee irrespective of mileage, a one-year guarantee on all replacement parts, a three-year paint

The larger KKK K26/70 turbocharger was installed on the 250bhp engine. Performance was dull below 3,500rpm, but electrifying when boosted.

Making a change from first aid kits and resuscitators, Porsche loaded the boot with Schwabian beer to prove the Turbo's capacity for life-saving.

warranty and a 10-year guarantee against rust holes.

The 944 Turbo earned itself a formidable reputation, but the introduction of the 16-valve 944S in August 1986 was not an unqualified success. The maximum power output of 190bhp (140KW) was positioned midway between that of the 944 (still 163bhp) and the 944 Turbo (220bhp) yet the performance felt wooden below 3,500rpm, and didn't really sparkle until 4,000rpm was passed. The maximum engine speed was raised from 6,500rpm to 6,800rpm.

All very well in Germany, grumbled the critics, but anywhere else in the world the owner would be well on the wrong side of the law before he could enjoy the advantages of 16-valve technology.

The maximum torque figure gave the game away, quoted at 230Nm (170lb/ft) at 4,300rpm, compared with the 944's 205Nm (151lb/ft) at 3,000rpm; at 3,000rpm, however, the 944S had only 200Nm (147lb/ft) and the advantages just weren't there below 4,000rpm. It was priced in Germany at DM58,950, or DM6,000 more than the 944 model, and in Britain at £24,000, or £2,300 more than the 944.

The main modification and point of recognition for the 1990 model year is the 928-style rear spoiler, which stands proud of the glass.

The 944S model had been previewed at the Frankfurt Show in September 1985, when a special Convertible Studie was seen for the first time. As it happened, a number of specialists had their own ideas about 944 cabriolets in other parts of the exhibition, but none was as attractive as Porsche's own. The styling was by Anatole Lapine and the car was built by Bauer to celebrate their 75th anniversary; they hoped, of course, to get the contract to build production versions, but would be disappointed.

Under the bonnet of this Studie was a prototype 16-valve engine developing 185bhp, a few short of the production version. The rear deck was enclosed, a change that entailed new sheet metal for the inner and outer rear wings as well as the addition of a lid, and the fast-looking soft-top was manually operated. Other features included Bosch ABS braking with negative offset for the front wheels, and an air bag restraint system in the new-style curved dash. The rear seat backrest was split, a feature that would go into production the following summer.

The 944S engine was conceptually identical to the latest 928S V8, virtually one half of it even to the same bore and stroke dimensions (100 x 78.9mm, capacity 2,479cc) now that the S was a full 5-litre. The intake and exhaust valves were arranged in parallel rows and operated by a pair of camshafts, the exhaust shaft positioned where the previous single shaft had been, and a short chain was used to drive the inlet shaft. The exhaust shaft was driven by a wider, stronger toothed belt running from the crankshaft, incorporating a mechanical tensioner.

The spark plug was now in the centre of the hemispherical combustion chamber, and with equidistant flame travel it was possible to raise the compression ratio to 10.9:1. Three knock sensors were incorporated into the heart of the engine, the Turbo model still having one so that it could be run closer to its knock limit on lower grades of fuel. Other features included a redesigned camshaft drive, an intake tract with magnesium passages, a new larger capacity oil sump and a revised exhaust system.

Floating calipers, like those on the 944, were retained for the S version, but the 944 Turbo's rear wheel brake circuit

Always ready for a new adventure, Gerhard Plattner drove a 944 Turbo with full three-way catalytic equipment a distance of 50,000 kilometres in 33 days. The trip, early in 1985, visited Nordic countries in winter, but was mostly in Germany, to prove that emission controls were compatible with high-performance cars.

The 16-valve 944S was introduced in August 1986 but was not the immediate success that Porsche's management hoped for. With a 190bhp engine it was a midway model between the eight-valve 944 and the Turbo.

pressure regulator was adopted to prevent locking-up in adverse conditions; the 944 Turbo, meanwhile, had ABS brakes as standard so it didn't need the regulator any more. From the outside, the only distinctions between the 944 and the 944S were the rear badges and discreet '16 ventiler' scripts on the sides, in front of the body protection mouldings.

If the 0–60mph figure is important, or 0–100km/h for Europeans, the 944S was a disappointment since the time was reduced by merely half a second compared with the 944. Porsche claimed 7.9 seconds for 0–100km/h, and *Motor* confirmed a time of 7.5 seconds from rest to 60mph. Sharp-eyed noters were surprised to see *Motor*'s time to 100mph, 21.1 seconds, which was actually a tenth slower than *Autocar*'s figure for the base-model 944 four years previously.

Surely the extra 27 horsepower should be easier to find? Well, the weight had gone up to 1,280kg, an increase of 100kg over the original 944, but only 40kg more than the more luxuriously equipped 'contemporary' 944 with standardized power steering. Effectively the advantage of the

Electrically operated seats were a popular option by the time the 944S was launched for the 1987 model year. Fore-and-aft adjustment was manual, however.

Performance of the 944S, customers soon realized, was no better than the eight-valve model's below 4,000rpm, and therefore at all legal speeds. Nice car, they judged, but not worth the extra money. Badged '16 ventiler', it accelerated to 60mph in 7.5 seconds and had a top speed of 142mph.

Customers have asked about proper sunroofs ever since 1976. There isn't enough area to have a wind-back roof, but since 1982 there has been an electric engagement to lift the rear surface . . . or the panel can be removed altogether.

944S was in its top speed, 228km/h (142mph) against 220km/h for the eight-valve model.

Road-testers and prospects alike regarded the 944S rather dubiously. *Motor* wrote about the 'exemplary top-end bite', which was indeed a key feature, something that made the S feel more sporty, and if we look back on the 2.5-litre 944S it should be stressed that it was a very fine, rewarding car, well up to the usual Porsche standards. Simply, it didn't offer the advantages over the normal 944 that customers would expect in the new-car market at the price premium demanded.

Porsches were, in any case, becoming rather expensive again: for the 1987 model year the factory raised its prices by an average of 6.5%, and the weaker relationships of the US dollar and £ sterling was beginning to cause grave difficulties in both these markets, and in Zuffenhausen.

There were rows in the boardroom, too, as the development of the 944 Cabriolet was discussed. Some board members wanted the car to be produced by Bauer, friends of Porsche since 1950, but Peter Schutz was adamant that the American Sunroof Company would do an equally fine job for

less money. He won the day, but the ASC had yet to build its factory at Weinsberg and the Cabriolet model was effectively delayed by two full years, to January 1989. When the contract was awarded, Schutz was moved to say that in future new Porsche models would be designed as convertibles from the outset and turned into coupes afterwards, to save all the problems (of interest, Lotus came to exactly the same conclusion before designing the new Elan).

There had been technical problems, too, in making the 944 Cabriolet's chassis stiff enough without the roof in place. ASC takes fully built 944S coupes from the line at Neckarsulm, removes the tops and carries out all the necessary panelwork, strengthens the chassis and installs the beautifully neat soft-top, including the electric motor operation, and lowers the windscreen and surrounds by 60mm. It is, necessarily, a lengthy and costly operation which adds £4,700 to the British tax-paid price.

On the racing side, the Porsche Turbo Cup competitors went into their second season, in 1987, with uprated 250bhp engines and with ABS brakes as standard, compulsory

Porsche's breakthrough with the four-cylinder range came with the 3-litre 944S2 model for the 1989 model year. It had virtually a new engine, rated at 211bhp, an excellent torque curve, and a top speed of 149mph.

Looks the same, but the 3-litre block is quite different inside, has reduced back-pressures on the down-stroke, and less coolant, which heats up faster. Each cylinder develops more than 50bhp!

A new front air dam is featured on the 944S2 with two low-down horizontal slats just like the Turbo. The rubber bumper pads have disappeared from this version. ABS braking is now standard on all Porsche models.

equipment. The engines were not far from standard, still with 2½-litre capacity and a nominal 8.0:1 compression ratio, but now had a larger KKK turbocharger and higher boost pressure, at 0.8bar (11.3lb). The Bosch Motronic chip was upgraded to suit, and power rose by 30bhp to 250bhp. Torque was increased as well, by nearly 15lb/ft to 258lb/ft at 4,000rpm.

Based on the previous year's competitions experiences, certain modifications had been passed into production cars, notably the more durable wheel bearings. As the racing programme continued to underline the strength and reliability of the Turbo model, so the demands grew within the factory for a more powerful road version.

Peter Schutz himself wanted to introduce the Turbo Cup specification to customers, and it has to be said that there was opposition from certain quarters at Weissach, where it was felt that perhaps production tolerances wouldn't allow the company to guarantee 250bhp. Eventually there was a compromise and a special series of 1,000 cars was announced. If they were produced to the high standard

expected, the specification could be consolidated.

High performance was the key of these 944 Turbo S models, with a maximum speed of 260km/h (161mph), a 0–60mph time of 5.6 seconds, and a 0–100mph figure in 13.5 seconds. By any standard, even that of the big brother Porsche 911 Turbo, the special 944 was very quick indeed, but a DM99,800 price tag in Germany (£41,250 in Britain) wasn't for the faint-hearted either. It was, by a substantial margin, the world's dearest four-cylinder car, but it also deserved a few more superlatives applied to its acceleration, top speed, handling and brakes.

As well as the full 250bhp engine, increasingly specified with full emission equipment, customers got an uprated five-speed manual transmission with a reinforced gearbox casing, the external oil cooler, a limited-slip differential as standard, improved four-piston fixed-caliper brakes, and disc-style 16inch forged alloy wheels, with 7J rims at the front (225/50 tyres) and 9J rims at the rear (245/45 tyres).

Underneath, the cars – all painted a metallic shade of rose pink – were suitably uprated with thicker front anti-roll bars

The American Sunroof Company won the contract to build Porsche's 944S2 Cabriolet, but it meant a two-year delay before the model went into production in January 1989. ASC took the completed cars to a new factory at Weinsberg to carry out the conversion, then returned them to Porsche for distribution. With a reinforced floorpan, the Cabriolet retains great torsional stiffness.

Styled by Tony Lapine, the Cabriolet has a new rear deck and wing design which looks extremely attractive from all angles. The hood is power operated and can be raised and latched within 15 seconds when the car is at rest. Fixed quarter-light windows were introduced to manage the airflow, and the Cabriolet is remarkably free of wind disturbance when open.

Exceptionally neat integration is the hallmark of the open 944, which has a lower windscreen than the closed car. A styling subtlety is the crease-line introduced around the rear flank beginning just above and behind the door handles. With the top raised, the Cabriolet is virtually as quiet inside as a coupe.

(1.2in diameter), uprated Bilstein gas dampers, heavier coil springs at the front and stiffer torsion bar settings at the rear. With the accelerator fully depressed the 944 Turbo S did have rocket-like performance, but the larger turbocharger (KKK type K26/70) took its own penalty. It was particularly noticeable in a high gear that there was little acceleration below 3,500rpm. There was little response to the throttle in fifth gear, even on a motorway at 90mph, but a shift down to third gear was rewarded by a tremendous surge of acceleration into the realms of the highly illegal.

Peter Schutz was right, but he wasn't in office to take the applause. Before the 1,000 cars had been sold around the world he'd left Porsche with his contract terminated, and deputy chairman Heinz Branitzki was installed in the chief executive's suite. The 250bhp specification was incorporated into the production line, and announced as the standard for the 1989

model year at a price lower than that of the special edition.

This was a busy time for the marketing department. In August 1988 Porsche's four-cylinder range underwent a thorough revision. The 160bhp 924S went out of production – the narrow body had lasted nearly 13 years and still had its admirers – and the standard 944 model went up in capacity to 2.7 litres, with the rather indifferent 160bhp power level of the 2.5 ('detuned' for a year to match the 924S) raised again to 165bhp. People could shrug their shoulders at the power rating, but the torque was very much more impressive at 225Nm (166lb/ft) at 4,200rpm, instead of 210Nm (154lb/ft) at 4,500rpm.

Porsche had, in fact, introduced a new cylinder block with wider bore spacings and 104mm bore dimensions, instead of 100mm. In conjunction with the usual 78.9mm stroke the 944's capacity went up to 2,681cc. We can dismiss the model quite briefly because it remained in production for one year

Contrasting interior trim is a recent introduction to the four-cylinder range, well illustrated in this European-specification Cabriolet.

only, disappearing in the summer of 1989 when the four-cylinder range was simplified in readiness for the move to Works V at Zuffenhausen. Still the 944 2.7 had a top speed of 137mph, and a slightly faster 0–60mph time of 8.2 seconds. When production ceased, there was no longer a 944 automatic in the price lists, but as already recorded, the Weissach engineers are working on a suitable auto transmission.

The Series 2 Porsche 944S was the real beneficiary of the new block, because the 104mm bore was allied to a new 88mm stroke, raising the capacity to 2,990cc. The limp performance of the 944S 2.5 was completely transformed as

the power went up to 211bhp at 5,800rpm, while the maximum torque figure increased to 280Nm (207lb/ft) at 4,000rpm.

Here was the high-performer the 16-valve 944S should always have been, with lusty mid-range performance, a claimed 0–100km/h time of 6.9 seconds and a top speed of 240km/h (149mph). *Autocar & Motor*, the combined weekly magazine, established a top speed of 146mph at Millbrook, but bearing in mind the earlier reservation about tyre scrub, the car would almost certainly achieve 150mph in good conditions. The 0–60mph time was established in 6.0 seconds, clearly ahead of the factory's claim, and the

US-market specification cars for the 1990 model year are equipped with this steering wheel containing an air bag.

0–100mph time was lowered to 15.5 seconds.

The new cylinder block was actually 4.5kg (9.9lb) lighter than the one still used for the Turbo, although stronger, with siamesed bores and 'closed deck' construction. It was also taller, allowing the 3-litre models a longer piston stroke, and at the bottom of the stroke there were openings between the cylinders which formed a gallery and allowed the downstroke back-pressure to be relieved. A plastic oil sump pan was fitted, for the first time in a production car.

Coolant water capacity was reduced by one-third, allowing a faster warm-up (something that's very important to passing the emission cycle test) and circulated more efficiently around the combustion chamber hot-spots and the exhaust ports. A considerable amount of work was done, too, on the management system, air cleaner, throttle, intake system (to feature pulse-effect charging) and exhaust, leading Herr Hensler to describe it as 'a basically redesigned four-valve engine'.

Unlike the Turbo model, the 3-litre 944S2 possessed great pulling power through the range, ample at 3,000rpm, but still sounded fairly happy as it neared the 6,400rpm maximum. Curiously, it seemed that every piston stroke could be heard at high revolutions, something that's laughed away by Jochen Freund: 'Think about it, each cylinder develops 53 horsepower, and that is what you can feel. It is not the mass but the power that you notice.' The new pistons, he points out, are lighter than those of the 2.5-litre so the decelerations are no greater.

There is scope, Herr Freund agrees, to go to 3.2 or even 3.4 litres with the 944S2 'but there are no plans to do so'. With a little imagination, though, one can foresee the arrival of a 2.7-litre, or even a 3.0-litre Turbo model.

The 944S2 went into production in January 1989, and at the same time the Cabriolet version became available. Porsche's four-cylinder range had now been simplified and consisted of the 211bhp 944S in coupe or cabriolet forms, and the 250bhp 944 Turbo, with UK prices between £32,000 and £39,900. All Porsche customers now had the benefit of ABS braking as standard, and there were no sluggards on offer.

Professor Bott, busier than ever in retirement, is a consultant to the company and his opinions are valued. 'The American market, particularly, is fickle and there is not so much loyalty. You must go on developing the car, introducing new features, and it must always be so advanced that your existing customer feels he *must* have it, he can't do without it! We know, because of the loyalty shown to the 911 and nowadays to the 928S, that the cars must be fast, very advanced technically, and rather exclusive.'

In July 1989, the 300,000th Porsche 'transaxle' car was made in Neckarsulm, a very high number in 14 years for such an exclusive marque. Of these, 137,500 were 924 and 924S models, and the annual average worked out at around 22,000 four-cylinder cars per year.

By the 1990 model year, production was way down from its previous high level to around 44 cars per day, equivalent to 10,500 per year, but they were all technocrats capable of running at 150mph or more on the autobahn. Porsche's

Cabriolet for the US market is externally distinguished by side marker lights and door rubbing strips.

Celebrations at Neckarsulm as the 300,000th Porsche four-cylinder transaxle car is produced in July 1989. The total includes all 924 and 944 models, and 13 years of production yields an average of 23,000 cars per annum. The contract was a good one for Audi and for Porsche!

management would, no doubt, be happy to see production rise to 60 per day, or 15,000 per annum, when the American market recovers, and these will be built by Porsche at Zuffenhausen in the new Works V.

Heinz Branitzki retired in March 1990 at the age of 61, having served the executive management for 18 years, and handed over to his successor a leaner, fitter company. Porsche's new chief executive, only the fourth in 19 years, was to be Mr Arno Bohn, formerly deputy chairman of Nixdorf Computers AG. He took over the reins at Porsche at the age of 42.

CHAPTER 5

924 and 944 in competition

Racing in Europe and the USA

The Porsche 924 model was active in competitions for only five years, from 1978 to 1982, and its achievements remain very much in the shadow of all the accomplishments of the six-cylinder models. These range from the 911's first GT success in the Monte Carlo Rally in January 1965 to the string of victories at *Le Mans* in the 1980s by the 956 and 962 racing cars. The 924 was only, ever, a stopgap model en route to the Porsche-engined 944 which made its debut in June 1981, and yet the road car was a commercial success and its exploits on the tracks were by no means inconsiderable, even if they were largely marketing-oriented.

Nobody at Porsche had ever remotely considered the 924 as a competitions model before a one-make series was devised by Porsche Cars Great Britain Limited, confined to British circuits in 1978, and there weren't even any homologation forms to refer to when the cars were prepared for circuit work. The series was inspired by John Aldington, then managing director of Porsche Cars Great Britain Limited, managed by the author (PR manager for PCGB at the time) and operated by the British Automobile Racing Club.

Although John Aldington might have shared his family's enthusiasm for motor racing (his father built up the AFN company almost from nothing, with the help of his brothers, and was a keen competitor of Frazer Nash cars) he kept his sporting inclinations firmly in check and even professed racing to be an unwarranted drain on resources.

It was something of a surprise, therefore, in November 1977 when he floated the idea of a Porsche 924 one-make championship, but Aldington's feet were firmly anchored to the floor. He saw it primarily as a marketing tool, and was among those who realized the need to get the 924 out on to the circuits and recognized as 'a proper Porsche'. In the previous eight months since the right-hand-drive model had been launched sales had been disappointing, and the 924 simply lacked image. Sales began to pick up substantially in the summer of 1978 – too soon to allow the racing championship much credit – and then continued to make progress.

Curiously, though, the 924's commercial success in America was in reverse since 13,696 had been sold in the 1977 model year, its first in the States, 10,483 in 1978 and 8,387 in 1979. It was an unwelcome trend which could be blamed only partly on the weak state of the dollar. Sales flattened out at around the 5,000 mark in 1980 and 1981, even though in an effort to *revive* sales in the USA the VW-Audi organization had 924s prepared for the SCCA racing series in '79. The diagnosis was the same as elsewhere, though: the 924 lacked image, and exposure in competitions might do it a power of good.

Tony Dron, equally accomplished as a racing driver and a journalist, was asked by PCGB to assess the 924 as a competitions car. He took a standard example from the demonstrator fleet to Castle Combe and in less than an hour had decided that it had the potential to behave well and safely on race circuits, and to entertain an audience. In January 1978 another test was conducted at Mallory Park, but this had to be cut short when the gearbox jammed in second.

Porsche's new, optional five-speed transmission was on its way in time to equip all the dozen cars that started the first race in April, although some of the competitors shifted straight from first to fourth and lost momentum rather quickly!

The 924's brakes were known to be weak, especially with drums at the rear, and the shortcoming was made worse by the fitment of special slick tyres made by Dunlop for the standard cast aluminium rims, the solid contact area clearly increasing lateral and longitudinal adhesion. Intelligent competitors drove around the problem, but others took a little longer to solve it.

The cars were remarkably standard, even to having full silencing systems. Aldington insisted on this as reinforcement of the 'showroom' appeal, but the approach of the cars was so quiet that many people felt they needed to make more noise to arouse the spectators. Power was increased by some 20% simply by means of polishing and blueprinting, from an

Since there were no GT races for which the 924 was eligible (or even homologated), a one-make series was arranged by Porsche Cars Great Britain Limited in 1978, in conjunction with the BARC. Artist Tony Matthews produced this publicity sketch at the end of '77.

A good grid was assembled for the opening round of the British Porsche 924 Championship at Donington. At last, the four-cylinder model had its track baptism.

The 924 Championship was won by Tony Dron, driving Gordon Ramsay's entry sponsored by Geoff Fox. Following him at Snetterton are Barrie Williams (JCT 600 entry), Gerry Marshall (Gordon Lamb Ltd) and Nick Faure (AFN Ltd).

Only once did a normally aspirated Porsche 924 take part in a World Championship race. Win Percy and Juliette Slaughter drove Gordon Ramsay's 924 Championship car in the Rivet Supply 6-Hour race at Brands Hatch in August 1979. They finished safely in 22nd place, winning the Group 4 category.

average of 99–101bhp at the rear wheels to a maximum of 120bhp, as measured on PCGB's rolling road at Reading.

A dozen dealers prepared cars for the series, which featured such colourful characters as Gerry Marshall, Tony Lanfranchi and Barrie Williams, but it was the rather more restrained personalities of Tony Dron (Gordon Ramsay Limited) and Andy Rouse (Heddell & Deeks) who dominated the results and the championship table. Prize funds of £1,000 per race were awarded by PCGB, the racing was exciting and there were no accidents of note, but even so the series closed after just one season.

British sales of the 924 had begun to pick up markedly in May 1978, and soon the dealers who had welcomed the series in January began to realize that they had neither the time nor the workshop resources to prepare the cars properly. There was a deal less enthusiasm to repeat the series in 1979, especially as only two drivers not supported by dealers had joined the series in '78, then had realized they were out of their depth and withdrawn. Without the support of the national dealer network there couldn't be a Porsche 924

Championship, so it was quietly abandoned.

Two dealers, AFN and Gordon Lamb, kept their cars intact with roll-cages and attacked British speed and endurance records at Snetterton in June 1979, the AFN car driven by Dron, Rouse and Percy also claiming the Commander's Cup, from Ford, for the greatest distance covered at the Norfolk track in 24 hours. The cars averaged 75.94mph (122km/h) over 2,000 kilometres (Gordon Lamb Ltd) and 77.31mph (124.4km/h) for 24 hours (AFN Ltd) at the only British venue to allow night-time running, but these records were beaten handsomely by other manufacturers later on when endurance record attempts were allowed at Vauxhall's Millbrook proving ground.

In January 1979 Juergen Barth, Porsche's racing customer liaison manager, tackled the Monte Carlo Rally in a 924. He and Roland Kussmaul, a Porsche engineer at Weissach, did well to finish in 20th place overall since they ran with a standard, 125bhp engine. The car was something of a hybrid since it was intended to be a 924 Turbo model with rear disc brakes and an uprated chassis, but a production delay meant

It looks like a 924 Turbo . . . but Porsche employee Juergen Barth had to settle for a standard 125bhp 924 engine for the Monte Carlo Rally in 1979 since the Turbo model's homologation papers hadn't come through.

A bare shell for the 924 DP (SCCA Class D, Production) series in the United States is photographed in Al Holbert's workshop towards the end of 1979. The SCCA-eligible cars were powered by 185bhp versions of the 2-litre engine, and had a prototype of the 924 Turbo suspension and brakes.

Typical of the 924 DP series was the Holbert-prepared kit car campaigned by Steve Pieper in 1980, seen here contesting one of the East Coast events in a car entered by Hugh Heishman.

Three days before the SCCA run-offs in 1980 Tom Brennan wrote-off his Herman+Miller 924 DP. A new car was rustled up from the Holbert race shop, rebuilt and raced at Atlanta over the weekend. In 1985 Brennan surprised himself and many others by winning the SCCA's GT-3 division in a similar car.

Doc Bundy, later a noted IMSA GTP driver, was Porsche's star of the SCCA's 1980 run-offs at Atlanta. Driving the Holbert Racing 924 he dominated the DP class from pole position. A year later Bundy was runner-up to Tom Brennan after his screen wiper failed.

that the turbocharged, 170bhp version couldn't be homologated until a week after the Monte ended. Later in the year Barth and Kussmaul took a 924 to Australia's tough Repco Rally where they won the 2-litre class and finished eighth overall.

Pressure from VW-Audi in the States resulted in the development of the Porsche 924 D-Production kit cars for the 1979 SCCA National series. 'Porsche Audi and its dealers were having some considerable problems in getting customers to believe that the 924 was a "true" Porsche', commented Josef Hoppen, the importer's competitions manager.

He selected the SCCA's National series as the springboard rather than the Trans-Am series as it would allow the 924 a better chance of success. Another advantage was that the special 924 model designed at Weissach could be produced in a limited series by Al Holbert at his workshop in Warrington, Pennsylvania. Also, rather than contest the entire SCCA series in 1979, it was only necessary to have cars ready for the run-offs (finals) at Road Atlanta in October.

Al Holbert, son of the Porsche dealer Bob, who had competed very successfully in Porsches in the fifties and sixties, had shown his abilities by winning consecutive Camel GT championships in 1976 and 1977 in Chevrolet Monzas, cars he prepared himself. He had tackled NASCAR and CanAm racing, and had also campaigned a 911 RSR and a 934, so his links with Porsche were already established and would become very important in the 1980s. Hoppen's plan was for Porsche to develop a kit version of the 924 and for Holbert to market them. Customers could buy these for $40,000, less only the windscreens, fuel tanks and tyres.

The capacity of the VW-Audi derived 924 engine remained at 1,984cc at the insistence of Hoppen, although the Weissach team announced that it was increased to 2,037cc, and new alloy pistons raised the compression ratio to 11.9:1. On the injection side a Bosch-Kugelfischer mechanical system replaced the K-Jetronic, and the power rose substantially from 125bhp to 185bhp at 7,500rpm. A 12-litre dry-sump oil system was used to protect the engine in racing conditions, and the weight of the factory-made 'DP 924' was reduced to 2,138lb (970kg) by the removal of fittings and door glass and the use of plexiglass for the rear side windows and the heavy rear hatch window. Holbert, though, was able to reduce the car's weight still further.

Underneath, the DP 924 had the new Turbo model's chassis with ventilated disc brakes at the rear, the 911's five-stud wheel fixings, and Bilstein gas dampers were specified. The wheelarches were cut and flared, with glass-fibre extensions, to accommodate BBS 7-inch wide, 15-inch alloy wheels.

The very first run, at Atlanta in October 1979, didn't look too encouraging as neither of the DP 924s reached the top 10, though at the time Holbert was still working on the handling; he reduced the spring stiffness drastically, softening the factory's 1,000/1,200lb spring settings to 350/280lb (front/rear) during the following winter. Eight of the kit-car models raced in SCCA events throughout 1980 and the series was eventually won by 'Doc' Bundy in the Holbert Racing entry, while fourth in the run-offs was Tom Brennan, who had wrecked his DP 924 while practising and had had it replaced by a totally new kit car in record time.

According to American Porsche expert Bill Oursler Holbert's 'kit' cars were reduced in weight to just 1,900lb

(861kg) by stripping out all non-essential items ruthlessly, even eliminating tabs and lugs on the shell that had no use in a racer (that would certainly help to explain why Holbert reduced the spring stiffnesses so greatly). The effort certainly seemed justified as Brennan won six regional races during 1980 and finished fourth in the finals, despite starting from the back of the grid.

In 1981, American interest focussed on the Porsche 924 Turbo model, but the finals at Road Atlanta featured another duel between Brennan and Bundy in their normally aspirated 924s. This time Brennan was the winner, in torrential rain that handicapped Bundy, whose wipers failed.

The Porsche 924 racing programme virtually ended there, although the surprising Tom Brennan popped up again at the SCCA's Road Atlanta finals in 1985 and won the GT-3 title, into which D-Production had been absorbed.

924 Carrera GT to Le Mans

It was difficult to get any reaction from Porsche's technical staff for exploits with the normally aspirated 924 model, nor even for the Turbo model. The 170bhp turbocharged engine absolutely transformed the 924, along with things like rear

May 1980, and the Porsche factory's Le Mans team of three 924 Carrera GTs is introduced at Weissach. Number 2 was the British entry, 3 was the American and 4 the German. Decorative liveries based on national flags were by the English stylist Arnold Ostler. Derek Bell is being interviewed alongside the British car; before the 24-hour race he switched hurriedly to the American car following Peter Gregg's road accident, to have his first race in partnership with Al Holbert.

Tony Dron and Andy Rouse just reached the finish in 12th place, on two cylinders with the engine seizing. Faulty mechanical fuel pump settings were blamed for exhaust valve failures.

Delayed in the night by a hare, Juergen Barth and Manfred Schurti were able to profit from teammates' problems and have their fuel pump settings rectified. They finished sixth overall, an amazing result for such a relatively low-powered car.

disc brakes and better suspension characteristics, but it wasn't taken seriously as a competition car once the Carrera version was introduced.

The 210bhp Carrera GT model appeared at the Frankfurt Show in September 1979, a real 'mean machine' in black or scarlet, with wide polyurethane wheelarches covering forged alloy 7J x 15in wheels (16in diameter wheels were an option). 'Carrera' lettering was embossed on the right-hand front arch and visually the model was in quite another class, as public demand for the 400 examples showed straight away. Still the capacity remained at 1,984cc, but an intercooler allowed more scope for engine development, and 210bhp was merely the stepping-off mark.

Dipl Ing Norbert Singer, a senior member of the Weissach engineering staff with responsibility for racing, was given the task of turning the Carrera GT into a fully fledged racing car. Before that he had been responsible for pushing the Appendix J regulations to their limits with the 935/78 model, the legendary 'Moby Dick', and he could be trusted not to miss any finer points of the rules.

The type 937 started with a production bodyshell which was then stiffened substantially with a complex aluminium roll-cage, and the exterior was clothed in new panels made of lightweight plastics, in much the same way as the 911 was transformed into a 935. The front bodywork was made more aerodynamic without losing the 924's appearance altogether, and the drag coefficient was held to a very reasonable figure of 0.35 (compared with 0.34 for the 924 Turbo and Carrera GT models) despite the use of drag's worst enemy, wide wheels with 11in section Dunlop tyres at the front and 12in section tyres at the rear. No attempt was made to fit a wing at the rear, and in fact the flexible spoiler around the rear plexiglass window was the same as that on the road version.

The front cross-member was welded in place to increase the torsional rigidity still more, and the MacPherson-strut front suspension system was retained, though with titanium springs, and Bilstein gas dampers were fitted; at the rear, though, the torsion bars were supplemented, as in the 935, with titanium coil springs which did most of the work. The driveshafts were made of titanium as well, coming from the

Still in its infancy, the 2-litre mechanically injected 924 turbo engine developed just 320bhp. This was enough to raise 170mph down the long straight, which proved barely enough to set a qualifying average for Le Mans 1980.

935 model, and the differential was fully locked.

By contrast, the engine was pretty straightforward, still the VW-based four-cylinder of 1,984cc. The KKK turbocharger was moved to the left side of the engine, the Carrera GT's intercooler was made larger and moved to the front, Bosch/Kugelfischer mechanical injection replaced the usual Bosch K-Jetronic system (this was almost the downfall of the works team at Le Mans), and dry-sump lubrication superceded the standard layout.

The power output rose by a fairly modest 50% from 210bhp at 6,000rpm in the case of the Carrera GT to 320bhp at 7,000rpm, while the torque value rose by some 40% from 202lb/ft (28.5mkg) at 3,500rpm to 282lb/ft (39mkg) at 4,500rpm. At the same time, though, the weight was reduced from 1,180kg (2,602lb) to just 930kg (2,050lb), and of course the car's performance improved dramatically. The important figure for Le Mans is the top speed, which rose from 150mph (240km/h) to 175mph (280km/h), with massive ventilated and cross-drilled brakes from the 917 and 935 racing cars to slow the 924s for the Mulsane corner.

Even so, the cars were barely fast enough to qualify. At Zuffenhausen and at Weissach there were some very mixed feelings about this trio of 924 Carrera GTR models, for there were dust sheets over the 936 Group 6 cars that were easily capable of winning the race (one did escape into the hands of Reinhold Joest and Jacky Ickx, but they had to settle for second place after having a broken fifth gear replaced).

The plan to run the four-cylinder cars was proposed by the marketing department and approved by Prof Dr Ernst Fuhrmann for exactly the same reasons that the 924 was competing in America . . . for greater exposure and acceptability. Fuhrmann knew, though, better than anyone else that in a year's time the 944 model would be announced, powered by Porsche's own engine, but he was no longer at the head of the company when that time arrived.

The factory's first plan was to run three cars driven by employees, so as to have the lowest possible profile, but following a suggestion from myself they were run in the national identities of Germany, Britain and America, with national drivers and tasteful national colours on the exterior panelwork.

The driver team was put into the shaker when Peter Gregg had a road accident near Le Mans and concussed himself, and test driver Gunther Steckkonig was admitted to hospital with a kidney infection. So Derek Bell switched to the American car with Al Holbert – it was their first shared drive in an amazingly successful partnership that lasted eight years – Porsche GB's 924 Cup leaders Tony Dron and Andy Rouse shared the British entry, and Juergen Barth and Manfred Schurti the German.

As everyone feared, the 924s were only just fast enough to qualify for the race, at between 4:10 and 4:17, in changing conditions, but the opening hour of the race raised everyone's hopes considerably. The first laps were driven in wet conditions, bad enough for driving normally but awful for racing. Bell kept the tops of the trees on the edge of his focus as he hung on to a fast bunch and was classified 16th overall after an hour, with Barth 22nd and Rouse 28th. Although they lacked power the front-engined 924s were ideal for the conditions, knifing through standing water, and even when the track dried they were still able to hold positions and then move up.

When the lights came on the three 924 GTRs were running 10th, 14th and 15th, and at breakfast time on Sunday the situation was better still as they lay sixth, seventh and eighth. Barth's car had been delayed half an hour when a rabbit ran across the road and broke the radiator, but no further damage was done and, with hindsight, this may have been a blessing. The two cars that had covered a greater distance began to misfire and lose power as the mechanical injection system shook itself to new, lean settings and burned the exhaust valves.

The diagnosis came in time to richen the mixture on the Barth/Schurti car, number 4, which continued at full speed to the end and finished in sixth place, a brilliant result for the car that barely qualified. The Bell/Holbert car, number 3, finished on three cylinders in 12th place and the Dron/Rouse car, number 2, expired on the finishing line with two cylinders operating, but in 13th place.

That was the first time the 924 model was entered by the factory in competitions, but the only follow-up was a single entry backing the Jules cars in 1981. There wasn't a ghost of

An interesting example of the 924 Carrera GTR, built in 1971. This was prepared privately by Schmidt Motorsport for world rally champion Walter Rohrl, whose contract with Mercedes-Benz had lapsed unexpectedly.

It was Professor Fuhrmann's idea that the 924 Carrera GT should represent the factory at Le Mans in 1980. With the drawing board number 937, the turbo model was extremely wide (72.9in) on account of the flares to cover the 11¾in wide BBS racing wheels, front and rear. The racing Carrera's weight was reduced to a stated 930kg (more likely 1,000kg) with the use of lightweight materials throughout, including titanium springs and driveshafts.

a chance of improving on sixth place at Le Mans, nor even of repeating it, Fuhrmann conceded – but early in 1981 the factory laid down a series of 59 GTS competition cars for sale, with 245bhp or 275bhp, at a base price of DM110,000, and a further 19 GTR models at DM180,000 with the full Le Mans specification and 375bhp.

As it happened these cars were slow to sell, although their values have since risen considerably. Racing customers certainly didn't have an easy time with them. At Le Mans in 1981, Richard Lloyd's car was troublesome and failed to qualify; another, run by the Almeras brothers, broke its gearbox after two hours, while the third, driven by Manfred Schurti and Andy Rouse, went the distance trouble-free. Although they covered one lap fewer than Barth's car the previous year they were classified 11th, their performance overshadowed by that of the factory's 924 GTP, in fact a racing prototype of the new 944 model.

Walter Rohrl, then the reigning World Rally Champion, drove the Porsche 924 Carrera GTR rally version in several European Championship events in 1981. His contract with Mercedes had gone badly wrong and the outings were arranged by Juergen Barth on a private basis to enable Rohrl to keep his hand in for the '82 season.

There was a higher-profile outing for Rohrl, though, as he shared the factory's 924 GTP with Barth at Le Mans, very successfully in fact, and drove it again at the Norisring a fortnight later. That was enough circuit work for Rohrl, though, as he much preferred rallies.

New Group B and C regulations came into force in 1982 so, understandably, the factory concentrated on the 956. The old 934 and 935 models were still eligible, and so was the 2-litre 924 GTR in a 'loophole' clause allowing IMSA-approved cars to compete in Group B. BFGoodrich, the American tyre company, made good use of this possibility at

A customer version of the 924 Carrera GTR was entered at Le Mans by Richard Lloyd in 1981 with backing from Canon, but it failed to qualify after running into engine problems. After a fierce argument in the paddock, Canon's Mick de Haas succeeded in getting his logos displayed on the factory cars!

Backing the 924 GTP (alias the 944 prototype) at Le Mans in 1981 was a works 924 GT, similar to the previous year's entry but with the uprated, 375bhp engine. Manfred Schurti and Andy Rouse could only finish 11th, although they covered only one lap fewer than the sixth-placed car in 1980.

The 1981 Porsche Carrera GTS/GTR model, available with engines rated from 245 to 375bhp. The GTRs had most of the factory mods, except for the titanium parts, but were slow to sell at DM180,000.

BFGoodrich, the American tyre company, entered the racing scene with a pair of 924 Carrera GTRs in 1982. One ran under the Herman+Miller banner, the other was entered by Brumos Racing, and both competed on street-legal BFG tyres. Highlight of the programme was an IMSA GT class win, and 16th place overall, at Le Mans in '82 for the Brumos car driven by Jim Busby and Doc Bundy. An interesting point, the bonnet-mounted air intake has been moved to the (facing forward) left side.

Le Mans in 1982 and 1983, the last appearances of the 924 model at the top level. The European GT Championship, incidentally, had long since died away, ended by Porsche's unchallenged dominance.

Although the factory had no immediate use for the 1980 Le Mans cars as they stood, they were put to good use. One had Porsche's own 2.5-litre, balancer-shaft engine fitted in 1981 and raced at Le Mans and at the Norisring, the second was entered privately at Le Mans for Schurti and Rouse (in the IMSA GT class, as it happened), while the third had a rather more interesting history on being shipped to the States after the 24-hour race.

This was the car that took Barth and Schurti to sixth place, and after the 1980 event it was shipped straight out to Al Holbert's racing shop at Warrington, Pennsylvania. There, the American was preparing to sell performance items to Porsche customers, and some of the factory car's features were assimilated into the SCCA and IMSA racers. Holbert, Doc Bundy and Rick Mears raced the car at Daytona in February 1981, the car managed by Porsche's Norbert Singer

but painted blue, with red and yellow trim. It looked a GTO class winner and performed like one until the head gasket failed. Paul Miller, though, had one of the first customer models and raced this to 22nd place overall and sixth in GTO, assisted by Skeeter McKitterick and Pat Bedard. By now the 924s were running with an improved, more efficient Kugelfischer injection pump and a higher compression, 7.1:1 instead of 6.8:1, and power was up to 375bhp though not, unfortunately, with the customary high degree of reliability.

Holbert Racing's Tom Seabolt continued to campaign the ex-works 924 throughout the '81 season, and alongside that he also ran a specially built 'semi tube-frame' 924 turbo. The cars weren't particularly successful, and late in the season they were sold to Bruce Leven's Bayside Racing team, ending the year in the hands of Leven and Hurley Haywood.

The BFG Tire Company supported two 924s in 1982 and one in 1983, equipping them with street-legal radial-ply tyres. One car so equipped was Paul Miller's, the other was run by Brumos Racing. The BFG Porsche team made an indifferent start to the season at Daytona and Sebring, two endurance

One-time CanAm specialists Ludwig Heimrath, father and son, campaigned a 924 Carrera GTR in the SCCA's TransAm series with some success. This is a US-built tube-frame example, a forerunner of the 944 Turbo GTR series built by Holbert.

events which should have suited the four-cylinder Porsches, but the whole programme was justified by an excellent result at Le Mans in June.

Still racing on production radial-ply tyres, Jim Busby and Doc Bundy took the Brumos Porsche 924 to victory in the IMSA GT class and 16th place overall, which allowed the American firm to reap full benefit in the publicity stakes. A wheel fell off the Herman Miller entry driven by Miller, Bedard and Schurti, taking a possible 1-2 class result out of the reckoning.

In 1982, Holbert Racing campaigned a full spaceframe 924 Turbo for Doc Bundy in the SCCA's Trans-Am series, netting victories at Sears Point and Portland. By now there were a number of customer cars in support, some being converted to spaceframe construction. An even better spaceframe machine was built by Tom Seabolt in Holbert's workshop for the '83 season, intended for Doc Bundy, but work stopped abruptly when Holbert became involved in the March-Porsche GTP programme, which turned out very successfully. The 924, ready to race, was sold to Paul Miller, who proved one of the quickest competitors in the GTO class, though lacking a win.

For the '84 season, Dave Klym, of Fabcar, improved Miller's 924 still further with double wishbone-style front suspension, enabling the owner to claim Trans-Am victories at Mosport, and at Lime Rock the following year. In IMSA, the 924 was moved down from the GTO class to GTU, giving it a new lease of life which Bruce Leven and co-driver Elliott Forbes-Robinson were able to exploit in their ex-Holbert car. They won the GTU category in the Daytona finals in 1984, and were runners-up to Mazda in 1985.

The 924 model was living on borrowed time now, and was effectively replaced in 1986 by the 2½-litre 944 derivation. The 2-litre model peaked early in competitions with that sixth place at Le Mans in 1980, but there was no real follow-up, and the car is not well remembered at Weissach.

Professor Bott, then director of research and development, has his own way of recalling the 924 programme: 'I like Black Forest cake. It has rich ingredients, chocolate, cream and cherries you know. But if I give you some sand and a bucket of water you cannot make a Black Forest cake that I would enjoy! It was like that with the 924. We did the best with the engine we had, but all the time we were thinking of the 944 which raced for the first time in 1981.'

A balanced programme

The car was entered at Le Mans as a Porsche 924 GTP, the P for prototype, and secrecy had to be maintained for two more weeks. Under the bonnet was a completely new engine of 2,479cc, with a massive bore of 100mm and a comparatively short stroke of 78.9mm. It was made almost entirely of aluminium alloys, had a 16-valve cylinder head and a KKK exhaust-driven turbocharger, and developed a comparatively modest 420bhp.

Anyone who'd had the chance to look at the engine properly would have been surprised to notice that it had twin counter-balancing shafts, of a type pioneered by Dr Frederick Lanchester and developed by Mitsubishi. Something else that was unusual for a racing car at Le Mans was the use of the latest Bosch Motronic engine management system with computer control for the injection, ignition mapping, fuel flow, boost pressure and knock sensing. It was a very sophisticated system far removed from the primitive mechanical injection system used on the previous year's 924s.

Otherwise, the car, which was driven by Juergen Barth and Walter Rohrl, looked much like the previous year's 924 Carrera GTR . . . not surprising, since the new engine was installed in a year-old chassis and painted up with Boss clothing sponsorship. The car now had thicker brake discs and weighed 998kg as scrutineered at Le Mans, but 950kg at the Norisring a fortnight later.

Testing at the Ricard circuit had been anything but encouraging as the engine was prone to mixing its oil and water after prolonged running, indicating a cylinder head gasket weakness on the open-deck block.

It should be stressed that the cylinder head was a one-off designed by Dipl Ing Hans Mezger and was nothing like the two-valve production head, nor even like the four-valve 944S head that came later. It had crossflow cooling, rather than a longitudinal flow, and the double overhead camshafts were driven by a belt from the crankshaft pulley to a pair of camshaft pulleys; the production four-valve heads had a belt driving one camshaft, and a chain across the valley driving the other in a fashion also adopted by Audi, and later by VW.

At one stage, Mezger persuaded Prof Bott to let him test the engine without the balancer shafts as a means of saving 5bhp. 'They came back to me a few days later,' Prof Bott recalls with satisfaction. 'They said we must have the balancer shafts because without them the vibrations are so bad that everything is breaking . . . the engine will only last a few hours.'

The engine was capable of producing 500bhp with 1.5bar boost pressure, and was rated at that figure when Rohrl drove the car at the Norisring at the end of June 1981. Endurance testing had been carried out with 1.3bar boost and 450bhp, and eventually the GTP model was raced with 1.1bar boost and 420bhp . . . and behaved beautifully for the whole 24 hours!

The prototype stopped 21 times for fuel and tyres, needed no mechanical attention at all, and droned along to seventh place overall in the classification. It also won a trophy for spending the least time in the pits, 56 minutes, and since fuel was metered in at a rate of 50 litres per minute and the tank

While BFG concentrated on the Herman+Miller 924 Carrera GTR, in 1983 Debbie Gregg – who kept Brumos Racing going after the death of her husband – continued to campaign her car in the IMSA series. Here at Daytona, she and Elliott Forbes-Robinson claimed the GTU pole in November '83.

Running at number 1, the 924 GTP made its debut at Le Mans in 1982. Under the bonnet was the unique 944 engine, turbocharged and with a 16-valve cylinder head, and detuned to a modest 420bhp. It ran without problems to seventh place overall, driven by Juergen Barth and Walter Rohrl.

held 120 litres it's hard to see how any time could have been saved.

In 1981, the 24-hour race was won by Jacky Ickx and Derek Bell in the Jules-sponsored 936, the last major victory for the old tube-frame Group 6 car, and there was a story behind that too. It had been the intention of Prof Dr Fuhrmann to compete only with production models, and Prof Bott confirms that Mezger produced the special 16-valve head so that the 944 would develop as much power as possible. 'Mezger's four-valve engine was never intended for production . . . but the production head was never intended for racing, either.'

Peter W. Schutz was appointed chief executive to the company on January 1, 1981 and he introduced new policies immediately. One of his first decisions was to resurrect the 936 and to win at Le Mans if possible; the racing department responded by installing the 2.65-litre, twin-turbo Indy engine, hitching it up to the ageing but 'bomb-proof' Can-Am four-speed gearbox and putting the body through a wind-tunnel again.

Ickx and Bell, too, had a perfect run to victory, and it was one of the finest endurance results enjoyed up to that time. The results were surpassed several times over in the Group C era, but no-one's thoughts had turned to that yet. At any rate, the pressure came off the 944 model as a potential racer, and when the Ricard test results were examined there was a strong lobby for cancelling the GTP's entry and concentrating on the two Jules cars.

Two races in the month of June started and ended the career of the so-called 924 GTP. Apart from any other consideration there was no class for the car in international racing, so the Porsche factory had to devise its own one-make series in 1985 to give the 944 Turbo worldwide track exposure. As usual it was the Americans who embraced the 944 as a competitions model, having both the SCCA and IMSA categories to accommodate the four-cylinder car.

The first appearance of the 944 Turbo production model was in America, in the Nelson Ledges 24-Hour race, Ohio, held in July 1984. The SCCA had been organizing 'the longest day' for five years and the '84 event attracted no fewer than 55 production car entries, all prepared in showroom condition complete with emission-free exhaust systems, showroom tyres, brakes, seats and even lights.

Porsche, though, took advantage of a new category for genuine pre-production cars, not 'prototypes' as defined by FISA but faithful in every respect to cars due for production within 12 months. BFGoodrich provided the tyres and picked up the tab, and the 944 Turbo was duly entered by Jim Busby, Rick Knoop and Porsche dealer Freddy Baker.

The car started from pole position ahead of Chevrolet Corvettes, Camaros, Mitsubishi, Nissan, even Saab Turbo and Maserati Biturbo models and proceeded to trounce the field, ending the race with a 42-lap advantage over the 'normal' 944 driven by Rick and Jamie Hurst and BFG engineer Bob Strange. Two more stock 944s occupied the fourth and fifth positions, just behind a Mazda RX-7 driven by John and Jeff Andretti. So far as the Americans were concerned there were no secrets about Porsche's 944 Turbo model, officially released in February 1985.

Times were changing in the States, as Porsche Cars North America was established in Reno as a wholly owned factory subsidiary in 1984, and shortly afterwards Al Holbert was named as PCNA's director of motor sports. He had become the leading IMSA driver with the recently introduced Porsche 962 model, his successes usually shared by Derek Bell, but he also identified the need for Porsche to regain its grip on the SCCA Trans-Am and IMSA GTO/GTU categories.

Spaceframe cars were now *de rigeur*, and Holbert turned back to the chassis now in Paul Miller's hands and regarded as the ultimate 924 racer. A new, similar spaceframe was made for the 944 Turbo engine and appeared as the 944 GTR at the SCCA's Road Atlanta run-offs in October 1985, with its engine modified to 525bhp by McLaren Engines in Detroit. The GTR was not competitive and during the winter the development was handed on to Alwin Springer, a former Porsche employee, whose Andial company is widely regarded as the best in the world of Porsche.

The main problem with the 944 Turbo engine was its inherent strength, according to Springer. 'Porsche builds things to last, making them tremendously strong. For us, we didn't need that strength so much as we needed more power since we were going to run these cars in sprints, not long-distance events.'

The more work that Springer did the more needed to be done, and he finished up with a power unit that was so far from original that it really needed the sort of development programme that only the factory could undertake. He used the 944 Turbo's original block and crankshaft, modified as for Le Mans in 1981, but had to work on the standard single-overhead-camshaft, two-valve cylinder head (which, Porsche experts stress, was perfectly adequate for a turbocharged engine). An entirely new management system was needed and caused the greatest problems, but eventually Springer had a 2½-litre turbo engine, with balancer shafts, producing at least 600bhp. Some believe that the engine actually produced, or could produce 675bhp, but that has never been confirmed.

Four-pad ventilated disc brakes were transferred from the 962 racing car, the driveshafts came from the 928, and the racing five-speed gearbox came from Hewland so this was a very sophisticated racing car intended for road car categories.

The weight was down to 906kg (1,980lb) but a considerable amount of lead ingot ballast, 320lb altogether, was needed to meet the SCCA minimum. In theory, such a car couldn't fail to be successful, but reality was something else. Problems with financing, in-house politics, continual rule changes from the SCCA, and the need for further mechanical development all conspired against the 944 Turbo GTR, and the only example to race in 1986 was handled by the two Ludwig Heimraths, father and son, but with only minor success.

The following year, the New Zealander, Bruce Jenner, formed a two-car team with Elliott Forbes-Robinson and secured backing from Olivetti. The 1987 season began well enough as EFR won at Brainerd, but that sent the SCCA's rules committee into session and the rules were so juggled that it became almost impossible for the car to succeed. Dave Klym was called in to modify the car so that it met the latest regulations, but at the end of the year Jenner crashed his GTR heavily in the IMSA Del Mar finals.

If the GTR's painful development was receiving any further help from Holbert, it was cut off when the Indycar project took absolute priority in 1988, and terminated when Holbert died, in his prime, at the controls of his light aircraft late in 1988.

So far as the Porsche factory was concerned, the only future for the 944 Turbo model in competitions was in the one-make series devised in 1986 and improved in every season that followed.

Turbo Cup thrills

As long as there was a Group B racing championship it was the playground of Porsche's customers, and the 934 (Group 4) model was the one that finally put the Grand Touring category to rest. In America the SCCA and IMSA guarded their GT series jealously, but elsewhere in the world FISA had better things to do. There was no series for the Porsche customers until the Zuffenhausen firm made its own.

The Porsche Turbo Cup series was announced late in 1985 for the following season and would comprise seven races on German circuits, each with a prize fund of DM45,000. As far as possible the cars would run in standard trim, the engines

A typical scene in the Turbo Cup series, May 1988, and three dozen drivers try to claim the lead at the Nurburgring's first corner. These competitors are still mastering the compulsory ABS brake equipment. They soon found that it enabled them to brake deep into the corners, reducing their lap times.

still rated at 220bhp, and the cars would race with the catalytic converter equipment in place, therefore running on lead-free fuel.

Scrutineering weight would remain 'standard' too, at 1,280kg. Whatever was saved by removing the interior trim, fitting a driver's Recaro racing seat and a plastic engine cover, was balanced by the installation of a full steel safety cage, halon 4kg fire extinguishers and Sabelt safety harnesses by the specialist Wilfried Matter. Lap times were much better than standard, thanks to lowered and stiffened suspension, and the use of Dunlop racing tyres on 16in diameter, 8J/9J forged alloy wheels.

The Turbo Cup cars were offered at a special price of DM78,900 to bona fide racing customers and 40 were made for delivery in March 1986, Porsche keeping two, which were offered to personalities.

As a matter of interest, the Turbo Cup cars never went near the Weissach research and development centre; they were made alongside the 'series' cars at Neckarsulm, taken to Matter's workshop in Bruchsal for special preparation and then stored by the customer department in Zuffenhausen until starter's orders were given. The series was supervised by Dieter Glemser, one of Germany's most respected saloon and sports car drivers on his retirement at the age of 47, and a Porsche works driver in 1966–67.

Close racing was guaranteed and the opening laps were a series of hair-raising encounters. After the competitors' first visit to the Norisring in June 1986, the fifth round of the inaugural series, there wasn't a car which hadn't collected damage and a couple were written off. In *Christophorus*, Porsche's superb house magazine, it was noted reprovingly that 'one has to wonder at how little responsibility some drivers feel for their 80,000 mark machines, not to mention those of their competitors'.

Roland Asch, who would become the star of the series over four seasons, won that particular event under intense pressure from Harald Grohs and Joachim Winkelhock, and the final round at the Nurburgring was won by Joerg van Ommen, from Grohs, in a contest that (according to *Christophorus* again) 'went to the outer limits of sporting legality'.

The worthy and popular winner of that first series was Joachim Winkelhock, younger brother of Manfred, who had died at Mosport 13 months previously when a tyre let go on his Porsche 956. Three drivers had stood to win the championship going into the final race, and in second and third places were Joerg van Ommen and Harald Grohs.

Porsche's Turbo Cup series went European in 1987 with extra races at Brno (Czechoslovakia), the Salzburgring (Austria), Spa (Belgium), Jarama (Spain) and Monza (Italy), with ten rounds making up the series.

Another series of 40 cars was built, more advanced technically with uprated 250bhp engines, ABS brakes and further improved suspensions. The price of the cars went up steeply to DM95,000, but the prize funds were increased to DM54,000 per event.

Modifications to the 2.5-litre engines were quite minor, in fact, but they had major effects. The KKK turbocharger was increased in size and boosted at a higher pressure, 0.8bar (11.28lb) and the Bosch DME digital management system mapping was adjusted accordingly. Power went up by 13.6%, from 220bhp to 250bhp at 6,000rpm, torque by 6% to 350Nm (258lb/ft) at 4,000rpm.

The car weight went up as well, mostly on account of the full 928S model brake system with ABS, to 1,350kg. Spring stiffnesses were further increased, the Bilstein gas-filled shock absorbers uprated, a thicker front anti-roll bar (3cm) fitted, the ZF power steering rack ratio raised, and the five-speed transaxle transmission was uprated (it already had an external oil cooler).

All told this made a very exciting track car which also had great possibilities for road use. Porsche's handout mentioned coyly that 'road approval is possible', but before long a series of 1,000 civilized road cars had been made, and after that the Supercup model became the standard Turbo model.

The performance was vivid: the Supercup model, equipped as standard with a limited-slip differential, would accelerate from rest to 100km/h (62mph) in 5.7 seconds, to 160km/h (100mph) in a creditable 14.5 seconds and cover the standing kilometre in 24.5 seconds, going on to a maximum speed of 260km/h (161mph). And the racing, needless to say, was more exciting than ever!

Porsche Club GB champion in 1989 was Steve Kevlin, driving the immaculate 944S2 prepared by AFN Ltd. In the 12 races that season Kevlin had eight class B victories and three second places. It was the first time the hard-fought championship, sponsored by BFG, had not been won by a 911.

The ABS brake system challenged the drivers' macho image and to begin with they all said they'd be better off without it. 'At first they switched it off', Jochen Freund confirms. 'They all smiled and said they could brake better without the system, but after a couple of races we noticed that they used it all the time. It's better on a dry track and far superior on a wet road. It just needs a different technique, that's all. The drivers found they could brake later, and right into the corner, without losing stability, so I don't think they'd like to be without the system now.'

Racing is always an important part of Porsche's test programme and Thomas Herold, the Weissach engineer assigned to the Turbo Cup series, tells of one problem that was detected on the circuits and remedied before any customers became aware of it.

'The drivers said that sometimes the ABS system didn't work for a moment, and we had to find out why this happened. The system requires a very even gap between the sensor and the rotor (brake disc) and we found that there was some flexibility in the system, allowing the disc to touch the

sensor. The wheel bearings were a little bit too weak so we made them stronger and increased the gap, and we did this to the production cars as well. There were no more problems after that.'

The 250bhp engine was itself developed in competitions and proved perfectly suitable for production, despite the reservations of some engineers at Weissach, who thought that the output couldn't be guaranteed in volume production. Shorter gear ratios, from first to fourth, were designed for the circuits and passed into production, along with a stronger differential; larger disc brakes, 282mm front and 289mm rear, came from the 928S4 model and were cross-drilled, with air ducting improved compared with the '86-model Turbo Cup cars. The clutch plate clamping pressure was increased and the plates themselves were glued, not rivetted to the backing, and this latter feature was not transferred to production.

Another technical advance perfected on the Turbo Cup cars was the all-metal catalytic converter, eliminating the costly and inconvenient ceramic honeycomb block which is

Steve Kevlin, the 1989 Porsche Club GB racing champion, made a piece of history in 1990 by defending his title with a 944S2 Cabriolet. An engineer with Porsche Cars Great Britain, Kevlin reckoned that the low-down weight of the Cabriolet would be to his advantage. The car was pictured at the BRSCC Racing Car Show, Olympia, in January 1990.

treated with a thin layer of platinum and rhodium. A typical ceramic cellular block has the surface area of two or three football pitches, vast in other words, but Porsche has found a way of making an equally efficient emission control unit simply out of treated sheet steel.

'If the layout is designed very carefully', says Jochen Freund, 'we can get lower resistance (back pressure) and better external aerodynamics.' It is certainly efficient, meeting US standards well enough to become standard equipment first in the 911 Carrera 4 model , and will be used across the range in the near future.

Switching to the Max Moritz team for his second season, Roland Asch enjoyed an excellent duel with Peter Oberndorfer and settled the championship at the final round, at the Nurburgring. Asch, who'd finished fourth overall the year before, notched up six pole positions, three wins and one fastest lap, an excellent record considering that all 40 cars really were equal in power, and frequently checked at Weissach.

Specifications were unchanged for the 1989 season, the last of the 944 Turbo Cup series and this time Asch really dominated the series having reverted to Paul-Ernst Straehle's team, with Joerg van Ommen as his nearest rival in the Max Moritz Porsche. Midway through the season the top cars were checked again at Weissach and found to give exactly 250 horsepower, with catalytic converters averaging 85% efficiency (compared with 90% for new equipment). This would meet the most stringent US standards with a good margin to spare.

And Roland Asch's reward? To be selected to drive a works-backed Mercedes in the 1990 German Touring Car Championship, alongside Alain Cudini in Dany Snobeck's team!

CHAPTER 6

Buying a used Porsche 924 or 944

What to look for

The principal appeals of Porsche products are design integrity, build quality, reliability and driving pleasure. It is probably safer to buy a 10-year-old Porsche from a reputable source than many other makes at five years, but prices inevitably reflect the advantages.

When Porsche extended the rust perforation warranty to 10 years, in 1985, it must have been reasonable to suppose that the monocoques would last a good deal longer than that. The warranty was extended, in fact, on past evidence, dating back to 1976 when the 924 model went into production with a steel body galvanized by the hot dip process. A six-year warranty was offered initially, applicable to the chassis, and this was extended to seven years in 1981, applicable to the entire car.

In the early days, the 924's roof panels weren't galvanized, and untreated stone chips at the front of the car tended to rust – even the metal air dam, and particularly the backs of the exterior mirrors, which were rapidly changed to the 911 style for the 1977 model year. It should be pointed out that the warranty did mean rust *holes*, not rust patches, and even stone damage didn't deteriorate that far within the warranty period.

There have been cases of corrosion on the early cars, built in the seventies, around the wings and centre rear panel (rear number-plate area), but the wings are bolt-on and relatively inexpensive, so rust in this area shouldn't be a complete turn-off. Corrosion is rare in cars younger than 10 years of age, but it should be noted that tail silencers wear out faster than centre silencers and piping.

Still referring to the early 924s, there are some more general pointers, although in all probability the problem areas have already received attention. The right-side engine mount was prone to fracture and this led to nasty vibrations, which could be felt through the pedals. Tight starter motor looms sometimes caused electrical shorting, non-starting and even led to the engine cutting out.

A loud whirring noise from under the centre of the car could be caused by a seized clutch spigot bearing. Still on transmission, if an incorrect oil is used the gearchange may stiffen up, and this symptom may also be caused, though rarely, if the linkage seizes up. If the clutch pedal seems too high it could be that the pedal stop has broken, and that entails removing the pedal box.

There was a modification to the original fuse box (1976–77) to prevent the fuse for the heated rear window burning out, but it's highly unlikely that this would have been neglected. On earlier cars the heater slide controls should be tested, as they sometimes seized and broke on right-hand-drive models. The water heater control valves were also prone to seizure on the cars of the seventies.

The VW-Audi-based 2-litre engine was generally extremely reliable, but the usual caveats apply to older, high-mileage cars. Exhaust valve guides were prone to wear out on hard-driven cars, and a very smokey exhaust would be the telltale. Exhaust manifold studs could fracture, especially if the engine has been misfiring and consequently vibrating. Any reduction in fuel pressure can lead to hot starting problems, but most older cars will have had a modification kit fitted. As

Inlet tracts and air-metering system are prominent under the bonnet in all versions: this is a 924S, with the Porsche engine replacing the 924's original Audi unit.

for the electrical fuel pump . . . don't worry, they always whined very audibly!

Cylinder head gaskets were prone to failure if the engine overheated, and such an event was usually caused by a failure of the electric fan to operate properly. Solenoids, connections and thermostats need to be checked annually.

The two most important areas are steering and brakes. As with any old car, the owner, or purchaser, should pay attention to steering column play. If there is excessive movement it will lead to an unpleasant rattle when the car is on the move.

The 924's steering rack, like the brake system, is of VW-Audi origin so is neither difficult to obtain, nor particularly expensive. The brakes were always the weakest part of the car, and the solid front discs were prone to wear. Even when the 924 was a young model customers were horrified to be told that their pride and joy needed new discs after 30,000 miles – or even 10,000 miles in hard-driven cars!

The discs could, in fact, wear out as quickly as the brake pads themselves. What was good enough for a VW Golf was not, frankly, good enough for a heavier, 125mph sports car. Similarly, the rear drums needed frequent adjustment to keep the pedal firm; automatic transmission cars were often heavier on brakes than manuals because they did more work despite the fact than they might be driven more in towns.

As will be clear from the descriptions in earlier chapters, these are far from the only Volkswagen parts used in pre-1985 924s and early 944s also have easily identified

Packed underbonnet area of a 944 Turbo, with another variation on the cast-alloy inlet tract theme. Maintenance should only be attempted by the well informed!

Golf/Scirocco peripheral components, from door handles to instruments and switchgear. The Porsche factory and their British off-shoot have never been keen to acknowledge parts commonality and it isn't easy to establish the exact equivalents from the VW-Audi parts lists. However, some specialists in parts for older Volkswagens and Audis may be able to identify and supply appropriate 924 parts – at cheaper-than-Porsche prices.

These cars should be watertight. Look for any evidence of leaks around the sunroof (this applies to 944 as well as 924). Drain tubes should be properly secured and kept clear, and they can be the source of persistent trouble in an unlucky car. Also, on earlier 924s, the drain tube in the rear wheel well locker could be squashed flat, which could lead to an unwanted lake forming. If the rear hatch windows are habitually pulled down by one corner the surrounding trim can break its seal, causing water leaks.

In the autumn, it's not unknown for occupants to get wet laps, though not regularly. It is important to see that leaves are not collecting in the bulkhead 'trays', where they could block the drain. Should this happen, enough standing water could accumulate to come out of the fresh air vents.

As we know, the early 924 Turbos (1979 and 1980 model years) were prone to having turbocharger problems, especially if the owner switched off while the turbine was running at full speed, or immediately afterwards. It was found that it paid to run the engine slowly for the last mile. Also, contemporary oils were not as good as later blends for

Seats may seem hard on first acquaintance but remain comfortable for journeys of long duration. They are durable, too, though lighter-coloured examples may reflect hard usage.

turbocharged engines, with their local hot-spots.

Some of these 'Mark 1' cars had problems with premature wear of their valve guides, cured in the 'Mark 2' by the use of better materials. Also, oil tended to seep from the turbocharger's flexible connecting pipes, and in all versions the exhaust manifolds tend to work loose, causing heat shields to rattle.

It was particularly important with the turbo engines to keep an eye on the water gauge, because of the higher temperatures involved. Regular checking of the radiator sender unit and the electric fan switch is strongly recommended.

The 177bhp 924 Turbos, of the 1981 and 1982 model years, were rather more reliable and are a very attractive buy even at the age of 10 years. The improved engine breathing, along with some other technical improvements, made the later ones much nicer to drive. The front wheel balance was very sensitive, and a change of tyre make could aggravate any imbalance. However, the last series made in the 1982 model year had the 944's steering and suspension components, and there were no further problems.

The 944 series has been free of endemic problems, but one over-riding danger on all versions is the failure to keep the oil level up to the 'High' mark. *The oil level must never fall below 'Low'.* These are sports cars and they tend to be driven hard, sometimes by people who neglect to check the oil level as frequently as recommended. Occasionally these people are faced with very expensive engine repair bills.

This condition was sometimes aggravated in the early 944s by oil seepage from the front of the engine, around the balancer shaft bearings, a problem which was cured by fitting better seals. Also, the early models were somewhat prone to cylinder head gasket trouble (oil in water) and even to difficulties with the unique oil/water intercooler, but these problems were ironed out after a year of production. Also, on the subject of levels, the power steering fluid level needs checking regularly to ensure that there are no leaks. If there are leaks from the 944's power steering system, the solution is likely to be expensive. Porsche's official line is that the seals at the steering rack are not replaceable, so that the whole rack assembly has to be replaced. An exchange scheme applies to the rack, but the price is still over £600.

Some 944s, even the Turbo models produced from 1985 onwards, have shown a tendency for their hydraulic engine mountings to soften, and the first symptom is engine vibration on tickover. Jochen Freund dismisses this as poor quality control by the supplier, claiming that the correct standard was reached by 1985. 'Our supplier could not build the dampers to a consistent standard', he says, 'and there was no way of finding out without cutting them open.'

The early 944 Turbos (1985–86) sometimes had a tendency for their clutches to judder, or to become heavy. This was a minor problem cured by attention to the release bearing and guide tube.

Though the pre-'S' 924s are in some respects less expensive to maintain than the 944, it is worth reminding

Rear seat accommodation is snug and, of course, nicely trimmed, but unlikely to appeal to adults for prolonged occupation.

Radio/cassette player mounting immediately ahead of the gearlever is not the world's most accessible.

that none of these are cheap cars to run. In the enthusiasm of discovering a secondhand Porsche for the price of a new Escort it is all too easy to forget that cars that were, and are, expensive when new incur correspondingly costly service and repair bills. Routine servicing – every 12,000 miles or once a year – costs around £500 a time at an official Porsche dealer and the marque's studied exclusivity is reflected in the prices of even the most prosaic components.

Porsche's dealer network tends to retail the young, expensive cars and offers an excellent warranty, following a 71-point check round the car. Also, the customer can buy an extended warranty, and need have no concerns about his Porsche ownership.

Older cars, say five years of age or more, tend to retail through non-franchised outlets, privately, or through the flourishing Porsche Club Great Britain (its magazine, *Porsche Post*, is a fine source of inspiration through the 'classified' pages, and of course members tend to be honest about their cars when selling to others).

Any prospective customer can ask the vendor to meet him

Cassette holder incorporated in the centre console between the seats on later models is a neat touch.

at a Porsche franchised dealership to have the used car checked over. Most will undertake this with a prior appointment, and AFN Porsche London, who supplied much of the information for this chapter, will give a used car a thorough check for a sum in the region of £100. This would seem to be a very reasonable outlay for peace of mind, when many thousands of pounds will change hands for a second or thirdhand sports car of unknown history.

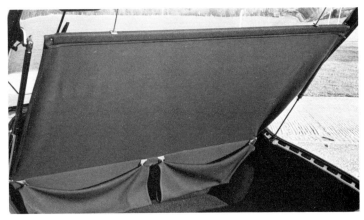

Roller blind, to conceal luggage from would-be thieves, and oddments bags are useful features of the rear compartment.

Comparison of 924S and 944 Turbo noses reveals evolutionary changes, but the retractable headlamps remain a distinctive trademark.

APPENDIX A

Milestones in the 924 and 944 story

1972 Volkswagen initiates the design of EA425, to replace the VW-Porsche 914 model.

1975 Porsche buys the rights to EA425 and prepares to launch it as the Porsche 924. The agreement is to build the coupe model in the Audi-NSU plant at Neckarsulm.

1976 The Porsche 924 goes into volume production. Total of 5,145 produced before the summer break.

1977 Total of 23,180 Porsche 924s produced by the end of the model year (July) making this the most successful model ever produced by the company. A special series of 'Martini' 924s is made, in white and with luxury trimmings, to celebrate World Championships in Group 5 and Group 6 racing. The automatic version is introduced for the 1977½ model, and a roller blind installed to hide luggage in the rear compartment.

1978 924's rear suspension mountings are redesigned with rubber bushes to reduce noise and improve the ride quality. Production of the 924 model passes 50,000 in just 26 months, but US sales decline by 3,200 to 10,483. Porsche's own five-speed gearbox is introduced as an option, and specified for all the cars competing in PCGB's 924 Championship, won by Tony Dron. The 924 Turbo model is announced with 170bhp, all-disc braking and many refinements sought by 924 owners.

1979 Audi's five-speed gearbox is standardized for the 924 going into the 1980 model year. The brake servo diameter is increased from 7in to 9in to reduce pedal pressure, there is an automatic light in the luggage compartment, and the window frames are painted black. This upgraded model is identified by a flap over the filler cap. At the Frankfurt Show in September the 924 Carrera GT is shown as a prototype study with a 210bhp intercooled engine and polyurethane front and rear wings. At Weissach, engineers are experimenting with a fleet of methanol-fuelled 924s, and with the high-compression TOP cylinder head design.

1980 Three Porsche 924 Carrera GTRs finish sixth, twelfth and thirteenth at Le Mans, and a special 'Le Mans' edition of the standard (125bhp) model is produced soon afterwards. Porsche announces that 400 of the Carrera GT models will be produced for sale; 200 will be sold in Germany and 75 in Britain, the remainder in other European markets. The corrosion warranty is extended to seven years on all Porsche models, and the 924 receives suspension improvements and extra soundproofing. 'Mark 2' 924 Turbo model is introduced with 177bhp by means of a smaller but faster-responding turbocharger, a higher compression ratio and digital ignition. Porsche's sales decline by nearly a quarter, led by cyclical decline in the US dollar and in December Prof Dr Ernst Fuhrmann's contract is terminated.

1981 A German-born American, Peter W. Schutz, becomes the chief executive on January 1, and introduces vigorous expansionist policies. The 911's future is assured and Porsche returns to Le Mans with a winning car. In seventh place, though, is an unusual Porsche '924 Prototype' racing with a turbocharged four-cylinder engine and counterbalance shafts. Two weeks after the race the 2½-litre Porsche 944 model is announced, already with a pedigree. The 924 Turbo goes into its final year with the 944's revised front suspension and steering components.

1982 Porsche announces in February that the 100,000th 924 has been made, in six years, and meets the terms of the contract made with VW-Audi in 1975; production continues. The 944 model goes into production, also at Neckarsulm, but with engines made in Zuffenhausen. With the discontinuation of the 924 Turbo model, the 924 has the same upgraded interior as the 944, the pu spoiler around the rear window, and more soundproofing. As production rises sharply, followed by profits, P.W. Schutz authorises a payment of DM5 million to be shared among the company's 5,350 employees.

1983 The 944 accounts for 51% of Porsche's production, which rises by an unprecedented 38% to 45,240 in the 1983 model year ending in July. Exports to America exceed 20,000 for the first time since 1977. Sales of the 924 model now exceed 130,000, but its markets are contracting. The 924 model benefits from the 944's electric-tilting sunroof (as an option) and an electric release catch for the rear window. New interior trim option is unveiled with the 'Porsche' name woven into the seat fabric. The backrest operation is made easier. The 944 model has the new options of power steering (a system almost identical to that on the 928S), electric tilt sunroof, and 16in diameter forged alloy wheels similar to those of the 928S; also 'sport pack' suspension becomes available with stiffer damper settings and thicker anti-roll bars.

1984 Going into its tenth and final year, the 924 has heated windscreen washer nozzles and a graduated-tint windscreen, features common to the 944. The start of the 1985 model year is delayed until October due to knock-on effects of the German metalworkers' strike which lost Porsche 5,660 cars. The year's production falls by only 1%, though, to 44,773. Porsche Cars North America is established in Reno as a 96% factory-owned subsidiary, to strengthen US representation. The University of Stuttgart confers the title of Professor on Dr Ferry Porsche. A Porsche model not yet announced, the 944 Turbo, wins the Nelson Ledges 24-hour race in Ohio by an amazing 42 laps.

1985 The 944 Turbo is announced in February with 220bhp, only 11bhp fewer than the 911 model and with similar performance. In July the last 125bhp, 2-litre 924 model is made, ending the run at 137,500, but for the 1986 model year it is replaced by the 2½-litre 924S model with a 150bhp version of the balancer-shaft engine. The interior is little changed, except for yellow numbering on the VW-originated instruments, but it does have 944-type suspension including new cast aluminium front suspension arms and rear semi-trailing arms. The 944 is substantially upgraded with many components from the Turbo model including the new-style curved dashboard with 928-style instruments, three-point attachments for the transaxle, larger sump and greater oil flow, a larger fuel tank and a quieter starter motor. Porsche's production tops the 50,000 mark for the first time, and half are exported to America. Financial turnover tops DM3 billion, another record, and heavy investments are made at Weissach and Zuffenhausen. The number of employees nears 8,000, including Weissach where the number of employees has doubled in five years to 2,045. All models have a two-year mechanical warranty and 10-year corrosion guarantee. At the Frankfurt Show in September a 944 Cabriolet Studie is shown with a convertible top and a 16-valve four-cylinder engine.

1986 The new Porsche 959 4wd model wins the Paris–Dakar 'Raid', but customers have to wait another year before deliveries begin. In Germany the Porsche 944 Turbo Cup series begins, featuring near-standard models with 220bhp and catalytic converters. For the 1987 model year the 16-valve 944S model is announced with 190bhp, but performance is little better than the eight-valve model's. ABS braking becomes an option for all four-cylinder models. A new 'sport' suspension kit becomes available optionally for all models, based on the Turbo Cup developments. Porsche's production reaches an all-time high of 53,600 as a second shift is introduced at Zuffenhausen, turnover exceeds DM3.6 billion and staffing rises to 8,300. A new paint shop is opened at Zuffenhausen at a cost of DM100 million. As the 1987 model year begins American sales turn down. The company's profits decline from DM120 million to DM75.3 million

1987 Porsche's range is rationalized for the 1988 model year. The 'narrow body' 924S is uprated to 160bhp, but the 944 goes down to the same power output. However, 160bhp is guaranteed for the emission-controlled models as well, a bonus for the American market. The Porsche Turbo Cup series cars have their engines uprated to 250bhp, and in the autumn Porsche announces that a special series of 1,000 944 Turbo S models will be made to a similar specification. As American sales decline sharply, PCNA chairman John Cook announces that he is negotiating with other European manufacturers to handle their distribution arrangements. In December Peter Schutz's contact is terminated nearly a year ahead of time. Deputy chairman and finance director Heinz Branitzki is appointed chairman.

1988 In April Herr Branitzki announces that turnover in four-cylinder models has fallen by 29.8%, and that of 911s by 12.7%, while that of 928s has risen by 6.5%. In the financial year ending July, Porsche build only 33,000 cars against 53,000 the previous year, and the number of employees is reduced by 1,000. In the longer term, Porsche will be happy to make 30–35,000 cars per year as a ceiling. In the spring Porsche's new DM125 million Works V is opened, modernizing the production at last. With two shifts Works V has a capacity of 120 cars per day, or 29,000 per year. In the summer, for the 1989 model year, the 924S model is discontinued; with a new cylinder block and a 104mm bore dimension, the 944 model goes up in capacity to 2.7 litres, and in power to 165bhp, and the 944S to 3.0 litres and 210bhp. The 944 Turbo is standardized with the 250bhp Turbo Cup series engine. ABS braking is standardized for the entire Porsche range, and is compulsory for the Turbo Cup competitors. An Englishman, Brian Bowler, replaces the Canadian John Cook as head of PCNA.

1989 In January the 944S Cabriolet goes into production, and proves popular. Three months later the board announces 'acceptable' financial results after one of the toughest years in Porsche's history. Turnover on the vehicle side has dropped from DM2.99 billion to DM2.53 billion on 29,017 sales, but earnings rise by 114% to DM54.2 million. Production of four-cylinder models has fallen by 14,270 (to 10,000 compared with 27,000 in 1985). In July production of the 944 model is discontinued and there is no longer an automatic transmission in the four-cylinder range. The 944 series is standardized with the 211bhp 944S, also available in Cabriolet form, and the 250bhp 944 Turbo. Production at Neckarsulm runs at 44 cars per day, the equivalent of 10,500 per year. There are celebrations at Neckarsulm as the 300,000th Porsche four-cylinder transaxle car is made. Professor Ferry Porsche celebrates his 80th birthday in September.

1990 Heinz Branitzki retires in March at the age of 61 after reporting a continuing recovery. He is replaced by Arno Bohn, 42, former deputy chairman of Nixdorf Computers AG. Ferdinand 'Butzi' Porsche, who styled the 911 model and went on to found the Porsche Design company, is appointed to succeed his father as chairman of Porsche's supervisory board. The contract with VW is due to expire in December, and production of four-cylinder models is to be shifted to Works V, Zuffenhausen, in January 1991.

APPENDIX B

Technical specifications – production models

Porsche 924

Into series production February 1976. Right-hand drive sales commenced January 1977. Produced, with refinements, until August 1985, when replaced by 2.5-litre 924S.

Engine: VW-originated LT 4-cylinder, water-cooled. Sohc, 2 valves per cylinder. Bore 86.5mm, stroke 84.4mm, capacity 1,984cc. Compression ratio 9.3:1. Bosch K-Jetronic fuel injection. Maximum power 125bhp (DIN) at 5,800rpm; maximum torque 121.5lb/ft at 3,500rpm.

Transmission: Audi 4-speed manual gearbox located behind differential in transaxle form. 20mm diameter driveshaft from clutch (behind engine) to transmission. Final-drive ratio: 3.44:1. VW automatic 3-speed transmission available from January 1977.

Suspension, brakes and steering: Independent front suspension with MacPherson struts, coil springs, lower wishbones, optional anti-roll bar. Independent rear suspension with semi-trailing arms, transverse torsion bars, optional anti-roll bar. Steering, Volkswagen rack-and-pinion, no power assistance. Brakes, 9.4in solid discs front, 7in drums rear, with servo-assistance. Wheels, 5½J steel, or optional cast aluminium 6J x 14in.

Chassis and body: Unitary all-steel monocoque, 2 doors. Zinc-coated steel construction with 6-year warranty against rust perforation. Service intervals 12,000 miles.

Dimensions: Length 166.9in; wheelbase, 94.5in; width 66.3in; height 50in; track front/rear 55.8/54.0in. Fuel tank capacity 13.6 gallons (62 litres).

UK price at launch: £6,999 including Car Tax and VAT. Extras included 6J alloy wheels (£264.42), stabilizer bars (£80.73), metallic paint (£230.49), automatic transmission (£450.00).

Model year developments:

1977   Limited-edition 'Martini' version. Roller blind covers luggage.

1978   Porsche's own 5-speed gearbox offered as an option. Rubber bushes specified for rear suspension mountings. Uprated shock absorbers. Electric windows offered optionally, also black-centre alloy wheels. Oval exhaust tailpipe, chrome-plated.

1980   Audi 5-speed gearbox standardized. Brake servo increased from 7 to 9in diameter. Automatic boot light. Cosmetic, 'black look' window surrounds, body-colour flap over filler cap.

1981   Corrosion warranty extended to 7 years, body fully galvanized, more soundproofing, front anti-roll bar standardized, stiffer rear torsion bars, indicator repeater lights on front wings, foglamp added at rear, air horns (from Turbo model) standardized. Optional 4-stud spoke-effect alloy wheels. Special model 924 'Le Mans' commemorates 924's 6th place at Le Mans, with spoke-effect alloy wheels, uprated suspension, Turbo-type polyurethane spoiler around rear window, reducing drag coefficient to 0.33.

1982   Improved interior ventilation, UK market standardized 911-type three-spoke leather steering wheel.

1983   Further lowering of noise levels, p/u rear spoiler standardized, 4 speakers built-in for radio system, synchromesh on reverse gear.

1984   In common with 944, option of electric tilt sunroof, electric interior release for rear window standardized, rear seat backrest release improved, new interior trim option with 'Porsche' woven into fabric.

1985   Graduated tint on windscreen, heated windscreen washer nozzles.

Porsche 924 Turbo

Into series production September 1978. Availability in UK delayed until September 1979 due to rhd conversion. Produced until summer 1982, phased out to make way for 944 model.

Engine: Based on 924 2-litre, but with new Porsche-designed aluminium cylinder head and KKK exhaust driven turbo-charger. Compression ratio 7.5:1. Bosch K-Jetronic fuel injection. Maximum power 170bhp (DIN) at 5,500rpm. Maximum torque 181lb/ft at 3,500rpm.
Second series (mid-1980 to mid-1982), compression ratio 8.5:1. Smaller KKK turbo with faster response, digital ignition, improved fuel economy. Maximum power 177bhp at 5,500rpm, maximum torque 184lb/ft at 3,500rpm.

Transmission: Porsche 5-speed gearbox located ahead of differential in transaxle form. 25mm diameter driveshaft from forward-mounted clutch to gearbox. Final-drive ratio, 4.125:1. Automatic not available.

Suspension, steering and brakes: Suspension systems as for 924 model but with uprated shock absorbers, stiffer rear torsion bar settings, reinforced rear trailing arms, 911-type 5-stud hubs, standardized front and rear anti-roll bars. Steering, Volkswagen rack-and-pinion, no servo. Brakes, 11.5in ventilated discs front, 11.4in ventilated discs rear, with servo assistance. Wheels, alloy, 6J x 15in.

Chassis and body: As for 924.

Dimensions: As for 924.

UK price at launch: £13,629 including Car Tax and VAT.

Model year developments:

1981 'Series 2' engine improvements and 177bhp. Siemens-Hartig digital ignition allows compression ratio increase to 8.5:1, economy improved by 13%.

1982 Improved interior ventilation, 928S-style 'slab' alloy wheels available optionally, 16in diameter, 50-series tyres. Model discontinued summer 1982 except for small number for Italian market.

Porsche 924 Carrera GT

Production limited to 406 cars in summer of 1980. Of these, 200 reserved for German market and 75 for British market. This series followed early in 1981 by 'evolution' version comprising 59 cars called GTS with 245bhp (1-bar boost pressure), and 19 GTR models for racing with up to 375bhp. GTR specification resembled that of works cars at Le Mans in 1980.

Engine: Based on 924 Turbo 2-litre, but with intercooler and digital ignition timing (DZV, introduced to 924 Turbo at same time). Compression ratio 8.5:1. Maximum power 210bhp (DIN) at 6,000rpm; maximum torque 206lb/ft at 3,500rpm.
GTS version, as GT except compression ratio 8.0:1; maximum power 245bhp at 6,250rpm; maximum torque 245lb/ft at 3,000rpm.
GTR version, compression ratio 7.0:1; maximum power 375bhp at 6,400rpm; maximum torque 299lb/ft at 5,600rpm.

Transmission: Porsche 5-speed gearbox located ahead of differential in transaxle form. Carrera GT, type G31/03. GTS and GTR, racing type 937/50.

Suspension, steering and brakes: Carrera GT and GTS, like 924 Turbo. GTR, racing components like Le Mans car (937). Wheels, forged-aluminium (Fuchs) 7J x 15. Optional forged aluminium 'slab' 7J x 16.

Chassis and body: Carrera GT and GTS, as for 924 Turbo but with polyurethane front wings and p/u flares on rear arches. The GTS had thinner sheet steel for unstressed body parts, aluminium for doors and bonnet, and less luxurious trim level.

Dimensions: Overall lengths: Carrera GT, 170in; GTS, 166.9in; GTR, 167.1in. Widths: GT and GTS, 68.0in; GTR, 72.8in. Weights: GT, 1,180kg; GTS, 1,120kg; GTR, 945kg.

Prices at launch: Carrera GT, £19,210 in UK including Car Tax and VAT; GTS, DM110,000; GTR, DM180,000.

Porsche 924S

This model succeeded 2-litre 924 model in September 1985. Porsche's 2½-litre, counterbalanced engine installed in 924's 'narrow' body though with 944's brakes and suspension incorporated (including cast-aluminium suspension parts instead of fabricated steel). The engine was 'detuned' to 150bhp, but in September 1987 was uprated to 160bhp. Model discontinued in August 1988.

Engine: Porsche-originated 4-cylinder, water-cooled, with twin counter-balance shafts. Bore 100mm; stroke 78.9mm; capacity 2,479cc. Bosch Motronic engine management. Compression ratio, 9.7:1. Maximum power 150bhp (DIN) at 5,800rpm; maximum torque 144lb/ft at 3,000rpm.

Suspension, brakes and steering: As Porsche 944. Wheels, 6J x 15in.

Chassis and body: Unitary all-steel monocoque, 2 doors. Zinc-coated steel construction with 10-year anti-corrosion warranty. Service intervals, 12,000 miles.

Dimensions: Length 166.9in; wheelbase 94.5in; width 66.3in; tracks front/rear 54.0/55.8in. Fuel tank capacity 13.6 gallons (61.8 litres).

UK price at launch: £14,985 including Car Tax and VAT. Extras included power steering (£499.58), rear anti-roll bar (£117.10), Panasonic radio system (£831), heated passenger door mirror (£29.57).

Model year developments:

1988 Power increased to 160bhp at 5,900rpm, maximum torque 155lb/ft at 4,500rpm, compression ratio 10.5:1.

UK price at launch: £21,031 including Car Tax and VAT. Extras included 3-speed automatic transmission (£959.30), air conditioning (£1,515), electric tilt sunroof (£1,008), 6Jx16 forged aluminium wheels with sport tyres (£2,022) and sports suspension pack (£735).

Porsche 944

Into series production January 1982. UK deliveries began May 1982. Incorporated Porsche's own 2½-litre, 4-cylinder engine with counter-balance shafts, developing 163bhp. 2-door coupe body widened at wheelarches to accommodate new 7J x 15in alloy wheels. Engine size increased to 2.7 litres for 1989 model year. Discontinued summer 1989.

Engine: All-aluminium slant-4, effectively half of Porsche's V8, 2 valves per cylinder. Bore 100mm; stroke 78.9mm; capacity 2,479cc. Compression ratio 10.6:1. Bosch Motronic engine management. Maximum power 163bhp (DIN) at 5,800rpm; maximum torque 151lb/ft at 3,500rpm.

Transmission: Audi 5-speed manual transmission, or VW 3-speed automatic with torque converter (£478 option), located behind differential in transaxle form. Final-drive ratio 3.89:1.

Suspension, steering and brakes: Independent front suspension with MacPherson struts, coil springs, lower wishbones, telescopic dampers and 21.5mm anti-roll bar. Independent rear suspension with semi-trailing arms, transverse torsion bars and 14mm anti-roll bar. Steering, ZF rack-and-pinion, no power assistance for early models. Brakes, front 11.12in ventilated discs front; 11.37in ventilated discs rear, with servo assistance. Wheels, 7J x 15in alloy.

Chassis and body: Unitary all-steel monocoque, 2 doors. Zinc-coated steel construction with 7-year warranty (initially) against rust perforation, extended to 10 years in 1985. Service intervals 12,000 miles.

Dimensions: Length 165.3in; wheelbase 94.5in; width 68.3in; height 50.2in; track front/rear 58.2/57.1in. Fuel tank capacity 14.5 gallons (66 litres).

UK price at launch: £12,999 including Car Tax and VAT. Optional equipment included air conditioning (£843), limited-slip differential (£385), sunroof (£350), fuel consumption gauge (£69).

Model year developments:

1983 Fuel economy gauge fitted as standard, interior trim upgraded, 4-speaker sound system installed.

1984 Power steering option, system almost identical to 928's, electric release for rear hatch and option of electric tilting sunroof, improved mechanism for rear seat backrest release, optional 'Porsche' weave upholstery, 'Sport' pack option of uprated suspension and thicker anti-sway bars, optional 928S-style 16in diameter forged-alloy wheels.

1985 Power steering standard, new 'telephone dial' 15in alloy wheel style adopted with forged-alloy 16in wheels 7J front/8J rear as options, heated windscreen washer nozzles, option of graduated-tint windscreen. February 1986, when Turbo version announced, 944 given new-style curved dashboard with 928-type instruments, vent air flow increased by 35%, central locking optional.

1986 944 gets Turbo's lighter, cast-aluminium lower front wishbones and rear semi-trailing arms, flush-mounted windscreen with radio aerial filament, UK-market wipers park on left, seats lowered by 30mm, steering wheel raised 18mm, electric seat height/rake adjustment option, battery moved to rear, fuse box and relays moved from passenger footwell to bulkhead; increased oil sump capacity, higher-capacity oil pump and enlarged oil galleries, starter motor quieter and lighter, alternator capacity increased to 115amps; fuel tank made of polyurethane, capacity increased to 17.6 gallons (80 litres), new fixings for transaxle at 3 points, option of full climate control and automatic speed control.

1987   ABS becomes optional, improved wheel bearings, sport kit option with stiffer springs, uprated shock absorbers, lowered ride height, heavier anti-sway bars, all from Turbo Cup experience

1988   Compression ratio lowered to 10.2:1, power reduced to 160bhp (DIN) at 5,900rpm, torque to 155lb/ft at 4,500rpm; same power figure available with full emission equipment.

1989   New block with 104mm bore increases capacity to 2,681cc. Compression ratio 10.9:1. Power output 165bhp (DIN) at 5,800rpm; maximum torque 166lb/ft at 4,200rpm, ABS brakes standard.

UK price at launch: £25,990 including Car Tax and VAT. 8-valve model discontinued August 1989.

Porsche 944 Turbo

Announced February 1985 with advanced turbocharged engine and intercooler developing 220bhp in 'world' specification, with or without emission equipment. New curved facia style introduced for 944. Turbo model has aerodynamic polyurethane front moulding with styling similar to 928S model, attention paid to underbody aerodynamics, and extractors provided at rear. Turbo Cup racing series in 1986 produces worthwhile benefits for production models. Power increased to 250bhp in 1988.

Engine: All-aluminium slant-4, 2 valves per cylinder, capacity 2,479cc. KKK turbocharger with water-cooled jacket. Compression ratio 8.0:1. Maximum power 220bhp (DIN) at 5,800rpm; maximum torque 243lb/ft at 3,500rpm.

Transmission: Strengthened Audi 5-speed gearbox, no auto

option, final-drive ratio, 3.37:1.

Suspension, steering and brakes: Suspensions as 944, having cast-aluminium front lower wishbones and rear semi-trailing arms, gas-filled telescopic shock absorbers, ZF rack-and-pinion steering with power assistance. Front and rear brake discs, 11.8in diameter, ventilated, ABS option. Wheels, cast-alloy 16in diameter, 7J front and 8J rear, optional forged-alloy 8J front and 9J rear.

Chassis and body: As 944.

Dimensions: As Porsche 944. Weight 1,350kg; fuel tank capacity 17.7 gallons (80 litres).

UK price at launch: £25,311.

Model year developments:

1987   (All 4-cylinder models), increase in brake servo ratio from 3:1 to 3.4:1 for lighter pedal pressure; improved wheel bearings accompany ABS braking as standard feature.

1988   Special series of 1,000 944 Turbo S models sold with Turbo Cup specification including uprated suspensions, larger KKK turbocharger and 250bhp output.

1989   Standard 944 Turbo SE uprated to 250bhp (DIN) at 6,500rpm; maximum torque 258lb/ft at 4,000rpm. Brakes have larger, 4-piston calipers. Wheels, forged alloy disc-type 16in diameter, 7J front and 9J rear.

UK launch price. £39,893

Porsche 944S

Introduced for 1987 model year with 4-valve per cylinder head, capacity remaining at 2,479cc. Compression ratio 10.9:1. Maximum power 190bhp (DIN) at 6,000rpm; maximum torque 170lb/ft at 4,300rpm. Power unit uprated to 2,990cc and 211bhp in S2 form, 1990 model year.

Engine: As 944, 2,479cc, with with 2 overhead camshafts and 4 valves per cylinder. Design almost identical to one bank of 928S4.

Transmission: As Porsche 944, with uprated Audi 5-speed transmission. No auto option.

Suspension, steering and brakes: As Porsche 944, ABS brake option, ZF rack-and-pinion steering with power assistance. Wheels, 7J x 15 cast-alloy front and rear, option of

Turbo-style forged alloys, 16in diameter. Weight 1,270kg.
Dimensions: As Porsche 944.
UK price at launch: £23,977 including Car Tax and VAT. Options included ABS braking (£1,844), forged-alloy road wheels (£1,849), sport dampers (£229).
Model year developments:
1989   S2 version with new block. Bore 104mm, stroke 88mm, capacity 2,990cc. Compression ratio 10.9:1.

Maximum power 211bhp (DIN) at 5,800rpm; maximum torque 207lb/ft at 4,000rpm. Full emission equipment now standard across range. ABS braking standard and suspension/brakes common to Turbo. Wheels, forged-alloy, 7J front, 8J rear x 16in. January 1989, Cabriolet version into production.
UK launch price: £31,304 including Car Tax and VAT. Cabriolet, £36,713 including Car Tax and VAT.

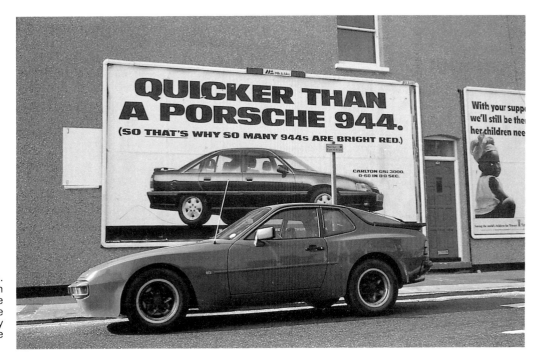

Trying to capture some prestige. But faces at Vauxhall were red when it was pointed out that the acceleration figures claimed for the Carlton GSi could be comfortably bettered by a Porsche 944. The advert was withdrawn rapidly!

APPENDIX C

Porsche 924 and 944 performance figures

Model	924	924 Turbo	924 Turbo	924 Carrera GT	924S	944	944	944 Turbo	944 Turbo	944S	944S2
Engine	1,984cc	1,984cc	1,984cc	1,984cc	2,479cc	2,479cc	2,681cc	2,479cc	2,479cc	2,479cc	2,990cc
Power	125bhp	170bhp	177bhp	210bhp	160bhp	163bhp	165bhp	220bhp	250bhp	190bhp	211bhp
Maximum speed	126mph	140mph	142mph	150mph	137mph	137mph	136mph	157mph	153mph	138mph	146mph
Acceleration (sec)											
0–30mph	3.2	2.6	2.6	2.2	2.5	2.5	2.5	2.3	2.2	2.6	2.2
0–40mph	5.3	4.0	4.4	3.3	3.9	3.8	3.6	3.4	3.3	3.7	3.3
0–50mph	7.4	5.4	6.0	4.2	5.4	5.3	5.1	4.5	4.2	5.5	4.5
0–60mph	9.7	7.0	7.7	5.4	7.4	7.4	7.0	5.9	5.4	7.5	6.0
0–70mph	13.6	9.0	10.2	7.1	9.7	9.9	9.4	7.8	7.1	9.8	7.8
0–80mph	17.7	11.3	12.7	8.9	12.3	12.7	11.8	9.8	8.9	12.5	9.7
0–90mph	22.3	13.8	15.9	10.9	15.9	16.8	15.4	11.9	10.9	16.4	12.4
0–100mph	30.4	17.9	20.4	13.5	20.1	21.0	20.0	14.9	13.5	21.1	15.5
Standing ¼-mile (sec)	17.2	15.4	15.7	n/a	15.7	15.6	15.7	n/a	n/a	15.7	14.4
4th gear acceleration (sec)											
20–40mph	12.1	10.0	9.6	9.6	7.2	6.5	6.8	9.0	8.9	7.8	6.1
30–50mph	11.0	8.8	8.0	7.9	6.7	6.3	6.7	7.7	7.3	7.4	5.9
40–60mph	10.8	6.8	6.4	5.9	6.5	6.1	6.7	6.2	5.6	7.4	5.8
50–70mph	11.0	5.4	6.1	5.0	6.3	6.4	6.4	5.2	4.5	7.5	5.5
60–80mph	12.5	5.5	6.4	5.1	6.6	6.7	5.9	5.0	4.5	7.5	5.3
70–90mph	15.7	5.9	6.9	5.3	7.1	7.1	6.5	5.1	4.8	7.8	5.3
80–100mph	19.9	6.4	7.6	5.8	8.0	8.3	8.1	5.4	5.3	8.5	5.8
Overall fuel consumption (mpg)	27.8	21.0	23.6	22.2	25.2	26.2	20.7	22.5	20.7	21.9	20.7
Kerb weight (kg)	1,044	1,204	1,180	1,180	1,164	1,195	1,320	1,258	1,350	1,280	1,310
Test source	*Autocar*	*Motor*	*Autocar*	*Motor*	*Motor*	*Autocar*	*Autocar & Motor*	*Motor*	*Motor*	*Motor*	*Autocar & Motor*
Date	12 Feb '77	26 Jan '80	25 Apr '81	26 Mar '88	7 Nov '87	29 May '82	28 Dec '88	6 Jul '85	26 Mar '88	26 Nov '86	29 Mar '88